What
Don't Let Scho

With a rich, historical backdrop, Darrow Miller immediately captivated my full attention in his latest book, *Don't Let Schooling Stand in the Way of Education*. Miller and his expert contributors provide a sobering analysis of our current education dilemma and how we got here. He does not stop there, though, but instructs and inspires with clear, biblical strategies that can once again turn the world upside down. This book is a must read for Christian parents, educators, and pastors!

Michael Myers, EdD
Director, School Leadership Program
Foundation for American Christian Education

Darrow Miller was introduced to Christian worldview thinking while teaching at L'Abri, a study center in Switzerland founded by Francis Schaeffer, who developed what is called "cultural apologetics," applying biblical truth to every area of life and culture. I became a Christian by studying at L'Abri and had the honor of meeting Darrow there. Now he has assembled a group of thinkers to offer insights on how to move beyond mere "religious" schooling and to embrace a rich and distinctive Christian worldview education.

Nancy Pearcey
Professor and scholar in residence at Houston Baptist University
Author of *Total Truth* and *Love Thy Body*

How timely is a book that explains so clearly why public education should not be the choice of Christian parents with so many families homeschooling who never thought they would because of COVID-19. This book so clearly explains what God considers education and the need for godly wisdom, rather than head knowledge. I would sum up the thesis of this book in one sentence: "God didn't call us to prepare our children for Harvard but for heaven."

J. Michael Smith
President, HSLDA (Home School Legal Defense Association)

Read this book! Now! Share it with three friends, and give a copy to your pastor!

Pete Talbott
Co-founder, Relief Factor

Education is one of the most important multi-generational topics at this time in history. Darrow Miller is one of the best authors to write on the subject, and to serve as the general editor with other amazing global educators and authors. What an important subject! What a team! What a book for this decade of transition, conflict, and destiny!

Loren Cunningham
Founder, Youth With A Mission
Co-founder, University of the Nation
Co-founder, Global Accreditation Association

This book is a clarion call for all Christians—not just educators—to develop a truly biblical worldview, in the midst of competing paradigms, philosophies and worldviews. Truly biblical education must include training the mind to think God's thoughts, so that we may become "salt and light" in the nations, equipped to implement Kingdom ways in every sphere of society that He calls us to. I highly recommend this book. It is not for the faint-hearted, but for those Christians who are serious about becoming nation-changers for God.

Darrell Furgason, PhD
Director, Worldview Studies Center
Former Adjunct Professor at the Jesse Helms School of Government
Liberty University

All parents want the best education for their children. *Don't Let Schooling Stand in the Way of Education* will confirm every parent's best intentions. The contributing authors are very persuasive due to their love of God, historical research, and insight to the human heart. This book is one of the best collections of reasons for Christian parents to rethink the purposes and goals of education I know of. I especially loved the clarification that school and education are not synonymous. The chapter on the history of education reminds us of our beautiful heritage of classical, Christian education. We are a great nation because we used to know the difference between education and school. The word *amateur* means *lover*. Parents are the kinds of amateurs we can trust to love children. *Don't Let Schooling Stand in the Way of Education* will continue the restoration of parent-led Christian education.

Leigh Bortins
Founder, Classical Conversations

Don't Let Schooling Stand in the Way of Education is a rich resource for parents and pastors who want to capture a biblical vision for a child's education. This invaluable book will help you think biblically about education with clarity, wisdom, and loving advice and avoid some worldview pitfalls in education. If you want your children to live for Christ in a fallen world as they thrive in their Christian walk, then this book will be an essential guide. I highly recommend it.

Josh Mulvihill, PhD
Executive Director of Church and Family Ministry, Renewanation
Author of *50 Things Every Child Needs to Know Before Leaving Home*

In a time when our nation and the church is facing a worldview crisis, this book is a must-read for every Christian parent and pastor. Miller and others address the issue of education biblically and show how biblical education must be taught in the home, church and school. Christians must understand how education shapes the beliefs, values and practices of society. Miller sounds the warning bell that all Christians must heed and act on before it is too late.

Dr. Glen Shultz
Founder and Director of Kingdom Education Ministries
Author of *Kingdom Education: God's Plan for Educating Future Generations*

Almost no one today can doubt that the educational standards of Modernity long ago succumbed to forces of disintegrating crisis. Indeed, crisis may be too mild a term. Thankfully, in this selection of trenchant essays collected and co-authored by Darrow Miller, a practical way forward is described and detailed—for parents and teachers alike. Herein is hope.

George Grant, PhD
Founder, Franklin Classical School

Now that Christian parents have had a year of COVID-forced online home schooling to find out what their children are actually learning, many are seeking alternatives. This book provides a map through the maze of modern schooling and calls for a return to God's ancient pathway of teaching and learning—one that nurtures the whole child, disciples him in the art of self-government, and prepares him for lifelong learning—to redeem the culture for Christ.

Stephen McDowell
President, Providence Foundation

Christian leaders, educators, and parents will find in this book solid ground for reflection on the true nature of education rooted in biblical principles. It will help you discern intentional deviations from these principles in history, and in society. It will help you to understand the essence of educating, and to reclaim its application in forging men and women that enable strong families and great nations. Be prepared to join this new reformation in motion!

Roberto Rinaldo, Jr.
Founder and President, AECEP (Association of Brazilian Principled Education Schools)

DON'T LET
SCHOOLING
STAND IN THE WAY OF
EDUCATION

DON'T LET SCHOOLING STAND IN THE WAY OF EDUCATION

A Biblical Response to the Crisis in Public Education

DARROW L. MILLER, GENERAL EDITOR

With contributions by Scott and Kimberly Allen,
Thomas A. Bloomer, Vishal Mangalwadi, Darrow L. Miller,
Christian Overman, and Elizabeth L. Youmans

Don't Let Schooling Stand in the Way of Education

Published in the United States of America by Credo House Publishers,
a division of Credo Communications LLC, Grand Rapids, Michigan
credohousepublishers.com

ISBN 978-1-62586-190-0

Cover design and interior typesetting by Jonathan Lewis
Editing by Donna L. Huisjen

Printed in the United States of America
First Edition

Other Books by Darrow L. Miller

Servanthood: The Vocation of All Christians

Discipling Nations: The Power of Truth to Transform Cultures, with Stan Guthrie

God's Remarkable Plan for the Nations, with Scott Allen and Bob Moffitt

God's Unshakable Kingdom, with Scott Allen and Bob Moffitt

The Worldview of the Kingdom of God, with Scott Allen and Bob Moffitt

Against All Hope: Hope for Africa, with Scott Allen and the African Working Group of Samaritan Strategy Africa

On Earth as It Is in Heaven: Making It Happen, with Bob Moffitt

The Forest in the Seed, with Scott Allen

Nurturing the Nations: Reclaiming the Dignity of Women in Building Healthy Cultures, with Stan Guthrie

LifeWork: A Biblical Theology for What you Do Every Day, with Marit Newton

Emancipating the World: A Christian Response to Radical Islam and Fundamentalist Atheism

Recovering Our Mission: Making the Invisible Kingdom Visible

Wisdom: The Way to Human Flourishing, with Gary Brumbelow

A Toxic New Religion: Understanding the Postmodern, Neo-Marxist Faith that Seeks to Destroy the Judeo-Christian Culture of the West, with Scott Allen

The proverbs of Solomon, son of David, king of Israel:

> To know wisdom and instruction,
>   to understand words of insight,
> to receive instruction in wise dealing,
>   in righteousness, justice, and equity;
> to give prudence to the simple,
>   knowledge and discretion to the youth—
> Let the wise hear and increase in learning,
>   and the one who understands obtain guidance,
> to understand a proverb and a saying,
>   the words of the wise and their riddles.
>
> The fear of the LORD is the beginning of knowledge;
>   fools despise wisdom and instruction.
>
> Hear, my son, your father's instruction,
>   and forsake not your mother's teaching,
> for they are a graceful garland for your head
>   and pendants for your neck. (Proverbs 1:1–9)

From John Milton's *Of Education*, "concerning the best and noblest way of education":

> Educations has a dual role: one *public*, to "fit a man to perform justly, skillfully, and magnanimously all the offices, both private and public, of peace and war"; and the other *private*, to "repair the ruins of our first parents by regaining to know God aright, and out of that knowledge to love Him, to be like Him, as we may the nearest by possessing our soul of true virtue."

This book is dedicated, quite simply, to all those parents, grandparents, and educators who want to see the children in their lives flourish in all their God-given potential and be equipped to be citizens who contribute to a free and flourishing nation.

Contents

Preface

Darrow L. Miller

This book was inspired by the overwhelming response to my September 9, 2013, blog post at Darrow Miller and Friends, *titled "School vs Education: The Difference Matters"* (darrowmillerandfriends.com/2013/09/09/school-vs-education/)*. Over the years, this article (edited for this book) has received more attention than the next top ten blog posts combined. Why might this be? Read on and you will see.*

School versus Education: The Difference Matters

Years ago, at L'Abri Fellowship in Switzerland, I heard Francis Schaeffer (1912-1984) say, "Don't let your children's schooling get in the way of their education."

To say that Schaeffer's comment (which was not original to him[1]) stunned me is not an overstatement. It started a process that ultimately transformed my view of learning.

Why was Schaeffer distinguishing between school and education? I had been to school. In fact, I had experienced more schooling than most people in the world, and more than many of my peers in the United States. I had completed many years of school (grammar and secondary school followed by university) and had then enrolled in seminary. I was the product of 19 years of formal schooling, to be exact. But I had not been *educated.*

First, although I had been an insatiable asker of questions as a child, eventually I had stopped asking. My schooling did not encourage an inquisitive mind, critical thinking, and creativity. Rather, I had learned to memorize and regurgitate what the teacher had taught me. My schooling was about facts and figures, rather than understanding, moral formation, virtue, and the adventure of exploring the world.

Second, I realized I didn't know how to think. *I had never had an original thought!* I grew up on comic books (images with few words). Today many children grow up with video games and TV (even more images and fewer words).

A third realization hit me while I was reading C. S. Lewis's Chronicles of Narnia, for the first time, at L'Abri. I distinctly sensed that I had not *lived* before that moment.

Fourth, I concluded that I had learned more in two months of informal study and work at L'Abri than in my nine months of formal seminary education.

Sometimes school and education go together. But often it's school *versus* education. Many young people who are thinking about college need to understand the difference. Many parents need to consider whether their children's schooling is actually interfering with their education.

While I had lots of schooling, I had little education. I came to understand the New Testament concept of repentance—*metanoia*—a fundamental change of mind. In that sense, I repented, realizing that my mind needed to be born again. This led to a number of other convictions:

- I needed to take responsibility for my education.
- I needed to be a lifelong learner, acquiring wisdom and knowledge from *all* of my life experiences, taking more opportunities to travel and meet people and learn from their lives and stories.
- I decided to always be in the process of reading several books simultaneously. Now I have a book with me to redeem the time whenever I'm waiting for someone or something.
- I needed to become a lifelong student of the Word of God, not just for my devotional life but for all of life, including my work.
- I needed to take words and ideas seriously. Over the years I have developed a great love of words, their definitions and histories/etymologies. This has brought me much pleasure.

The direction of my life changed as I considered the observation, "Don't let your schooling get in the way of your education!"

What did Schaeffer mean by this statement?

Education is lifelong. It doesn't happen solely in a classroom, during a structured period of time, or just via formal instruction. Education can take place anytime, anywhere, in the middle of a full life, in formal and informal ways. It occurs in the midst of creation, while we are navigating our way through society, when we are enjoying family and friends, as we engage with culture, and while we are in the marketplace and public square. Education points us to the cultural trinity: truth, beauty, and goodness.

Sometimes, unfortunately, *schooling* can stand as a barrier to children learning, growing in wisdom and understanding, and becoming educated in knowledge and virtue.

Neither word, I admit—*schooling* or *education*—is found in the Bible. As Elizabeth Youmans points out,[2] the words found in the Scriptures that relate to education are *teach*, *learn*, and *disciple*.

Studying the words *schooling* and *education* using Webster's 1828 *American Dictionary of the English Language*[3] and the *Online Etymology Dictionary*[4] yields fascinating results. More importantly, it confirms the distinction that Francis Schaeffer made.

Schooling

The *Online Etymology Dictionary* defines school as a "place of instruction." In 1828, Webster similarly defined *school* as a place where instruction occurs. Here is his primary definition of the word:

> SCHOOL, *noun* [L. schola; Gr. leisure, vacation from business, lucubration at leisure, a place where leisure is enjoyed, a *school*. The adverb signifies at ease, leisurely, slowly, hardly, without labor or difficulty. . . . This word seems originally to have denoted leisure, freedom from business, a time given to sports, games or exercises, and afterwards time given to literary studies. . . .]

The school is where "leisure is enjoyed," a place free from work. Literary studies take place *after* schooling. The idea of "'students attending a school' is attested from c. 1300; sense of 'school building' is first recorded 1590s." (*Schooling*, meanwhile for Webster, simply pointed to instruction, compensation for instruction, or reprimand.)

Education

While *school* denotes a building, *education* means the formation of a life. Webster defined *education* as follows:

> EDUCATION, *noun* [L. educatio.] The bringing up, as of a child, instruction; formation of manners. *Education* comprehends all that series of instruction and discipline which is intended to enlighten the understanding, correct the temper, and form the manners and habits of youth, and fit them for usefulness in their future stations.

Note that *education* is comprehensive. It deals with both the gaining of knowledge and the development of character—virtue. And the combination of virtue and knowledge leads to wisdom.

The *Online Etymology Dictionary* dates the word *education* to 1530 and defines its use as "child-rearing." This comes "directly from Latin *educationem* (nominative *educatio*), from past participle stem of *educare*." From 1610 the word was used "of education in social codes and manners; meaning 'systematic schooling and training for work.'"

The words *schooling* and *education* have very different meanings.

- The former relates to a place—a building, a place of leisure separated from work itself and from the preparation of a person for work.
- The latter is a process of instruction that prepares the mind with knowledge and understanding, the heart with virtue, and the will with wisdom. It prepares people for life and work.
- School versus education: the modern world has lost this distinction.

Since hearing this distinction from the lips of Francis Schaeffer, I have become a lifelong learner and have reflected much on the difference between schooling and education. Here are some of the distinctions I have discovered:

School	**Education**
A classroom with four walls	The world is my classroom (Job 12:7–12; Proverbs 25:2;)
Twelve years of primary and secondary school with an end date at graduation	Learning that takes and lasts a lifetime and beyond . . . even in eternity we will be learning!

Learning by rote: memorizing and regurgitating information	Forming an inquisitive mind, reasoning from principle, kindling creativity and imagination, thinking independently
Pursuing the latest fads and feeling good about oneself	The timeless pursuit of truth, beauty, and goodness
A quest for data, information, and technique	A quest for: knowledge—perceiving what the information declares understanding—discerning what the information means wisdom—applying the truth (moral application)
Responsibility of the state	Responsibility of the parents and the student
Foundation of Atheism	Foundation of Judeo-Christian Theism
Preparing people for tasks and behaviors in a consumer society; preparing for a job	Preparing people for life
Teacher focused	Student focused

John Milton (1608–1674), the English civil servant and brilliant poet whose works include the epic poem *Paradise Lost*, penned a classic Christian philosophy of education, stating:

> The end of learning is to repair the ruin of our first parents by regaining to know God aright, and out of that knowledge to love him, to imitate him, to be like him.[5]

These words and concepts from another era are highly relevant today. Don't let your schooling stand in the way of your education!

As you begin your journey through the book, please note the study guide that follows Chapter Seven. If you are interested in using a study guide to direct your reflections as an individual or as part of a small group discussion, please turn now to page 163 to orient yourself to the study guide feature. There you will find a brief introduction about how to use the study guide along with the guides themselves. In most cases there are several guides for different sections of the chapters. Please also note the symbol SG throughout the text. This marks a new guide for the next section of the text.

Introduction

Darrow L. Miller

This book is about education. SG-Intro

It is meant to alert parents and students about how poorly they are being served by the educational establishment, which is expending little to no effort to prepare young people for life, for a calling, and for being citizens of a free nation. It has done even less to help us reimagine the current monopoly of state-sponsored, illiberal education.

As a North American who has traveled, studied, and worked in 120 countries for half a century, I have experienced a public, state-run "education" from grammar through graduate school (having received a master's degree in higher and adult education). I am also an orthodox Christian who served for almost forty years with an international relief and development organization, witnessing the dismal results of educational systems in some of the world's poorest countries. Instead of equipping students to be creative and free human beings, their educational systems often employed a rote approach that stifled their imaginations and analytical impulses, training them simply to comply with the dictatorial rule of their leaders.

Their experience is no outlier. Most schooling today is simply the dissemination of information by the teacher and the repeating back of that information by the student. Little is done to prepare people for their life and work.

As we saw in the preface, schooling and education are not the same things. Education is rooted in the pursuit of truth and virtue; it leads to freedom. Schooling, at its best, is rooted in a search for a job and the reduction of a human being to a good consumer in a materialistic culture and subservient to a central government.

The Crying Need

As I have traveled the globe, I have witnessed nations abundant in resources yet living in poverty, nations of beautiful people enslaved by corruption, nations with bright children languishing in ignorance. How can this be? Why this wasting away? Much of the problem is rooted in the absence of true education, learning that builds on the naturally inquisitive minds of children, that draws out their uniqueness. Too often it is a state-run, state-imagined industrial "education."

Education in my own country too often is little more than a state-run system that has abandoned virtue, lacks an understanding of and commitment to the foundations of our free country, and has no long-term vision of preparing our children to live as free citizens of a constitutional republic. Instead, the system, based on postmodern ideology, prepares "yes people" to support an increasingly tyrannical society flirting with socialism, a society that systematically reduces human beings made in God's image to mere producers and consumers of material products.

Many parents, forced by the COVID-19 pandemic to get more involved in their children's education at home, have been shocked by what is being taught by the "educational professionals" in their local public schools. Indoctrination over issues such as Comprehensive Sexual Education, to take just one example, undermines what many children are learning at home or in the church. Some mothers and fathers have decided that their homeschooling situation will become permanent. Others are looking for private school options. Growing numbers believe the dominant system is broken.

In an October 2019 article in *The Atlantic* titled "When the Culture War Comes for Your Kid," George Packer, an award-winning journalist and the father of elementary school-aged children, writes of his painful personal experience struggling to navigate the New York City public school system circa 2019. His article provides a sobering, detailed picture of what is happening in the classrooms of our children. What he describes is coming soon to public schools across the United States and around the world. For many schools, it has already arrived.

Perhaps the most alarming part of Packer's article is how he reveals that our public schools are not religiously neutral. Rather, they are openly and explicitly inculcating a particular atheistic and postmodern worldview or ideology in their young charges. Here's how Packer describes the core tenets of this unbiblical belief system:

> Instead of equality, [the ideology] sets up a new hierarchy that inverts the old, discredited one—a new moral caste system that ranks people by the oppression of their group identity. It makes race, which is a dubious and sinister social construct, an essence that defines individuals regardless of agency or circumstance.[1]

Packer opens the curtain, allowing us to observe what is happening daily in his children's classrooms:

> [Our son had] been painfully aware of climate change throughout elementary school—first grade was devoted to recycling and sustainability, and in third grade, during a unit on Africa, he learned that every wild animal he loved was facing extinction. "What are humans good for besides destroying the planet?" he asked. Our daughter wasn't immune to the heavy mood—she came home from school one day and expressed a wish not to be white so that she wouldn't have slavery on her conscience. It did not seem like a moral victory for our children to grow up hating their species and themselves.
>
> I wished that our son's school would teach him civics. By age 10 he had studied the civilizations of ancient China, Africa, the early Dutch in New Amsterdam, and the Mayans. He learned about the genocide of Native Americans and slavery. But he was never taught about the founding of the republic. He didn't learn that conflicting values and practical compromises are the lifeblood of self-government. He was given no context for the meaning of freedom of expression, no knowledge of democratic [ideals] . . . or of the instruments with which citizens could hold those in power accountable. Our son knew about the worst betrayals of democracy . . . but he wasn't taught the principles that had been betrayed. He got his civics from Hamilton.
>
> [In our son's fifth-grade year, the] curriculum included the Holocaust, Reconstruction, and Jim Crow. The focus was

> on "upstanders"—individuals who had refused to be bystanders to evil and had raised their voices. It was an education in activism, and with no grounding in civics, activism just meant speaking out. At the year-end share, the fifth graders presented dioramas on all the hard issues of the moment—sexual harassment, LGBTQ rights, gun violence. Our son made a plastic-bag factory whose smokestack spouted endangered animals. Compared with previous years, the writing was minimal and the students, when questioned, had little to say. They hadn't been encouraged to research their topics, make intellectual discoveries, answer potential counterarguments. The dioramas consisted of cardboard, clay, and slogans.
>
> But the country's politics had changed dramatically during our son's six years of elementary school. Instead of hope pendants around the necks of teachers, in one middle-school hallway a picture was posted of a card that said, "Uh-oh! Your privilege is showing. You've received this card because your privilege just allowed you to make a comment that others cannot agree or relate to. Check your privilege." The card had boxes to be marked, like a scorecard, next to "White," "Christian," "Heterosexual," "Able-bodied," "Citizen."
>
> A teacher in Saratoga Springs, New York, found a "privilege-reflection form" online with an elaborate method of scoring, and administered it to high-school students, unaware that the worksheet was evidently created by a right-wing internet troll—it awarded Jews 25 points of privilege and docked Muslims 50.
>
> Carranza [our son's school] has mandated anti-bias training for every employee of the school system, at a cost of $23 million. One training slide was titled "White Supremacy Culture." It included "Perfectionism," "Individualism," "Objectivity," and "Worship of the Written Word" among the white-supremacist values that need to be disrupted.[2]

With the rise of postmodern culture, students are being taught that Western civilization is the source of the world's problems and needs to be deconstructed. And they are being given the tools to replace truth with narrative, reality with delusion, and reason with irrationality. As a consequence, we are witnessing Europe and North America falling apart morally and spiritually.

Under this scheme of indoctrination, students are largely imbibing economic Marxism from modern ideology and cultural Marxism from postmodern ideology. Many see themselves as citizens of the world, no longer citizens of their own countries. They know little of their nations' histories and seem unconcerned about this.

While public schools are naively assumed to be neutral when it comes to issues of worldview and values, they are founded on atheistic, postmodern, and neo-Marxist assumptions and thus promote moral and cultural relativism rather than virtue. It is no wonder that we see so much gross failure by otherwise well-intentioned educators.

Christian Overman of Worldview Matters often asks Christian parents, "Would you send your child to a Hindu school?" The answer is a resounding "No!" "Would you send your child to a Buddhist school?" Again, the answer is "No!" "Would you send your child to an Islamic school?" Again, the answer would be "No!"

Finally, he asks, "Would you send your child to an atheistic school?" There is an uncomfortable silence. Globally, most Christian parents unthinkingly send their children to state-run schools, naively assuming they are "neutral" in their worldview, educational philosophy, and moral code. They are not. They are atheistic in their ideology and amoral in their framework.

Societies shaped by the Judeo-Christian worldview and biblical principles have cut themselves off from their historic roots and are gradually experiencing a moral and spiritual breakdown. As chaos and corruption grow, societies are close to committing cultural suicide. Too often, therefore, modern and postmodern curricula are a gross waste of time and money, as young people graduate from these schools burdened with debt and ill-equipped for life.

So, why have I written this book? For three reasons.

First, in my extensive travels I have witnessed the need not just for schools but for education. Constructing school buildings is easy. They go up relatively quickly. Volunteers and donors can take pictures and feel satisfied. But the buildings need to be furnished, administrators and teachers hired. Someone must decide what will be taught and how it will be taught. Too often, the teaching is done by rote, and the students parrot what the teacher says. Too often, the system fails to teach them to think critically, ask questions, discover, and reason from principles. They may or may not get prepared for a job, but certainly they do *not* get ready for life. They are ill-prepared to provide leadership in solving community and national problems.

Second, as a product of Western state-run schooling, I am a perfect example of someone who was not prepared for life. I was taught to slavishly engage in a consumer society. Schooling in the West only prepares people for jobs. It does not prepare them to become citizens who can lead free and prosperous nations. Don't believe me? Only *37 percent* of U.S. high school graduates have attained sufficient proficiency in reading and math to matriculate into college.[3] And these numbers are falling.

Third, in many countries parents or churches start "Christian schools" in order to counter what is happening in the state-run schools. They hire Christian teachers, hold chapel services, and teach classes on the Bible. They assume, tragically, that this constitutes a Christian education. These elements may form a *religious* education, but they are not a *Christian* education.

Unfortunately, few Christian schools have built their theology of education from the foundation of a biblical worldview. Too often, what they offer is a secular education wrapped in a blanket of religious (evangelical or charismatic) terminology.

Most Christian schools operate from an unquestioned belief in the sacred-secular divide, in which spiritual truth has nothing to do with our everyday lives (a philosophical idea formulated in the Enlightenment). The Bible is merely one part of the curriculum, not foundational to it. Thus, many godly teachers unknowingly teach Christianity as an overlay on a humanistic education. While well-intended, these schools prove wholly inadequate to the task of true education.[4]

Worldview and Culture

What do these three reasons have in common? They fail to account for the role that worldview and culture play in language and education. Secularist leaders in academia today consciously ground education in atheistic assumptions. Humanist John Dunphy writes in his essay "A Religion for a New Age,"

> The classroom must and will become an arena of conflict between the old and the new—the rotting corpse of Christianity, together with all its adjacent evils and misery, and the new faith of humanism.
>
> I am convinced that the battle for humankind's future must be waged and won in the public school classroom by teachers

> who correctly perceive their role as the proselytizers of a new faith. . . . These teachers must embody the same selfless dedication as the most rabid fundamentalist preachers, for they will be ministers of another sort, utilizing a classroom instead of a pulpit to convey humanist values in whatever subject they teach, regardless of the educational level—preschool day care or large state university.[5]

In the West, universities founded to pursue truth and virtue and educate for life and freedom now push for a postmodern goal: the end of Western civilization. Much, if not most, of what passes for education in the West is simply indoctrination into thinly disguised economic Marxism and cultural Marxism, identity politics, moral and cultural relativism, and political correctness. We are producing a new generation of "social justice warriors" who hold to what the late Francis Schaeffer described as "arbitrary absolutes," today more popularly called "dogmatic relativism." Parents, students, teachers, and others grasp that something is terribly wrong with today's state-run and religious schooling, even if most of them can't put their finger on it.

As the American culture has changed, so has our educational system. With the rise of Darwinism, we have lost the sense of a moral universe and thus the loss of the development of virtue and moral character. With the rise of postmodern culture, the educational system has abandoned reason and reality; feeling and emotion are all that matter. An educational system without morals, reality, and compassion produces young adults without the ability to know who they are, why they are here, and how to govern themselves. This is why we see lawlessness and anarchy growing in our society. We are at a tipping point in our history. Thus, the profound warning of Dennis Prager, the Hebrew scholar, social commentator, and founder of Prager University: "To save America from the Left's destruction, take your kids out of public schools."[6]

Further afield, traditionally animistic societies—which hold a "belief in innumerable spiritual beings concerned with human affairs and capable of helping or harming human interests"[7]—often ignore the impact of animism on their educational systems. At the same time, they simply borrow secular education from the West without analyzing the impact of atheistic ideology.

In either case, education has not occurred until it results in an enculturation of the student into what is true, good, and beautiful.

Language and Culture

Another critical issue in education, not surprisingly, is language. Language both reflects and shapes culture. Both modernism and postmodernism have redefined words (e.g., *marriage*) and introduced new words (e.g., *autogynephilia*) as tools to de-form culture.

Animistic cultures, for their part, are trapped by words that hinder human flourishing. For example, many African dialects have no word for "future." In many world cultures, the female is called a slave or a tool, not a human being equal in dignity to her male counterpart, as the Bible affirms. Just what kind of impact do you think these deficient understandings would have on human flourishing in these cultures?

By contrast, languages rooted in Scripture create free, compassionate, and flourishing societies. Thomas Cahill helps us understand the significance of words through the biblical witness:

> The Jews gave us a whole new vocabulary, a whole new Temple of the Spirit, an inner landscape of ideas and feelings that had never been known before. Because of their unique belief—monotheism—the Jews were able to give us the Great Whole, a unified universe that makes sense and that, because of its evident superiority as a worldview, completely overwhelms the warring and contradictory phenomena of polytheism. They gave us the Conscience of the West . . . The Jews gave us the Outside and the Inside—our outlook and our inner life. We can hardly get up in the morning or cross the street without being Jewish. We dream Jewish dreams and hope Jewish hopes. Most of our best words, in fact—new, adventure, surprise; unique, individual, person, vocation; time, history, future; freedom, progress, spirit; faith, hope, justice—are the gifts of the Jews.[8]

Noah Webster understood that language is an indispensable unifying agent for a nation. "Language is the expression of ideas, and if the people of one country cannot preserve an identity of ideas they cannot retain an identity of language." Webster also said, "A national language is a band of national union."[9] Webster recognized that a nation's freedom requires the language of freedom, language founded in biblical principles.[10]

Elizabeth Youmans explains Webster's motivation to create the first dictionary for a free people:

> At the age of fifty, Webster tackled the writing of the first American dictionary, a task that required the mastery of 26 languages. He wanted to provide the new nation with her own dictionary. He understood that words are the building blocks of ideas. The colonies had fought eight years to win independence from England in order to be self-governing under God. Webster believed it was important to provide definitions that communicated the worldview of the U.S. Constitution and its underlying Christian principles of liberty and civil governance. In addition to researching the root meanings of words, he also researched words in the Hebrew and Greek lexicons and defined them according to how they were used in Scripture. Some of his entries have as many as twenty definitions based on the fine nuances of meaning found in the Bible! . . . Webster's 1828 is the only dictionary in the world that includes biblical meanings of words.[11]

As Webster intended, education should prepare students to live in the midst of the created universe, before the face of God, thereby helping to build nations of wisdom and virtue. To truly *educate* our children and grandchildren, we need to think theologically about education. Doing so will allow us to lay the foundation for tomorrow's free, prosperous, compassionate, and just nations.

An early advocate of Christian schools, Mark Fakkema, understood the challenge, writing, "If we are to meet our educational challenge we need an all-embracing, unified Christian philosophy. To formulate such a philosophy is our greatest need today in the field of education."[12] But how do we accomplish this?

Rather than start from scratch, let's lean on Christians from the past who have already done the necessary deep thinking and developed a theology of education that we can adapt in our current context. These Christians produced a workable, but largely forgotten, theology of education during the Protestant Reformation in Europe 500 years ago. The fresh intellectual winds of the Reformation encouraged God's people to begin thinking theologically in every area of society, including science, economics, politics, social policy, and education.

In this book I will demonstrate a model of education carried by the Reformation into Europe and to the American colonies by the Puritans. This approach founded Harvard, Yale, Princeton, and other key institutions that laid the foundations for the most free, just, and prosperous nation the world has ever seen.

We will explore the nature of this theology of education, the system it produced, and why it has been abandoned. We will then outline what we must do to restore or build principled education across the globe. As Webster has written,

> Every civil government is based upon some religion or philosophy of life. Education in a nation will propagate the religion of that nation. In America, the foundational religion was Christianity. And it was sown in the hearts of Americans through the home and private and public schools for centuries. Our liberty, growth, and prosperity were the result of a Biblical philosophy of life. Our continued freedom and success are dependent on our educating the youth of America in the principles of Christianity.[13]

My Intention

My intention with this volume is not to create a theology of education. That would require a whole series of books—and besides, it has already been done.

My intention instead is to delineate the need to reform educational systems and concepts globally and to promote the Puritan concept of *technologia* as a rich theological model for education today.

My intention is to call Christians to think biblically about education and to develop educational opportunities in their homes, communities, and nations based on biblical principles.

The Plan of This Book

In addition to my focus, which you will find fleshed out in Chapter One, this book seeks to answer a series of questions on the vital overall theme, through the insights of trusted experts and colleagues who have been studying in this area for many years.

Where is education grounded in order to raise up free, self-governing citizens?

A growing percentage of the world's population is children under age 25. Tragically, many of these children are abused and abandoned. They are undervalued and often despised. Abortion kills millions more every year. All of us can clearly see the often deplorable behavior of adults, parents, and societies toward children. But what is the underlying cause of this abuse and neglect? The roots are found at a cultural level, where children are seen as burdens, and these attitudes are driven by secular and pagan ideologies. Beginning to restore the dignity of children will require a biblical understanding of the child. In Chapter Two, Dr. Elizabeth L. Youmans lays the groundwork by helping us see "The Christian View of Children."

What was the nature of early education in the founding of the United States, perhaps the freest nation ever to exist?

The Bible profoundly affected the practice of education in colonial America, from grammar school through university studies. Dr. Youmans's excellent treatment of the subject in Chapter Three, "The Remarkable Role of the Bible in Early American Education," describes the contributions of several of the nation's founders and prominent early leaders.

What happens to Christian education when Christians and societies abandon the Judeo-Christian worldview?

Indian scholar Vishal Mangalwadi provides a provocative answer in Chapter Four, "Seminary: Education or Religious Schooling?" Vishal argues that when Christians worked from a biblical worldview, they established universities that offered a comprehensive and integrated education. But when Christians adopted the sacred/secular dichotomy of the Enlightenment, they eventually abandoned the formation of universities for the building of Bible schools.

Why do so many Christians fail to see the connection between the Bible and their work?

As Dr. Christian Overman points out in Chapter Five, "Why Education? The Lost Purpose for Learning," the answer is simple: Most of us have lived through an entire educational experience that makes virtually no connection between God and math (or science or economics). Such an education can produce only a dualistic mindset. But this approach is not necessary. With remarkable clarity, Dr. Overman leads us through the diagnosis and suggests a way forward.

What kind of impact does this kind of education have on the home, the "smallest nation"?

In Chapter Six, "Prayerfully Consider Home Education," parents Scott and Kimberly Allen share their personal journey, as they discovered that parents have the ultimate authority and responsibility for educating their children, not the state. Theirs is a fascinating story of their applying the concepts in this book to home education and the wonderful and dynamic changes that took place in their family as a result of this decision. After all, the family is the bedrock of any society. Healthy families are foundational to healthy nations.

What kind of impact does this kind of education have on the building of a city or a nation?

In Chapter Seven, "Calvin and Geneva: Nation Building Missions," Tom Bloomer takes us on a historical journey through the city of Geneva as a model of what God can do when we work with Him to disciple a nation. The city's history, including the ministry of its greatest disciple, John Calvin, provides us with both examples of great success and some important warnings.

May this book help all of us to consider what we can do in the grand and vital task of helping turn our societies back to a biblical understanding of education to form virtuous and wise self-governing citizens of a free nations. Please enjoy your journey!

ONE

Schooling versus Education

Darrow L. Miller

Every narrative has a beginning. The opening line of a narrative launches the storyline. The storyline, or plot, creates the framework for the characters in the story. This is true not only of written stories but of cultural narratives as well. SG-1a

While competing narratives exist that claim to explain the place of human beings in the universe, the true framework for humankind is revealed in the Bible. What's the opening line of the biblical narrative? "In the beginning God created the heavens and the earth." That opening statement creates the framework enabling us to understand all of life. Therefore, it guides our understanding of education, the pursuit of truth, and the life of free and responsible human beings. How so?

Let's note first of all that the biblical narrative begins with God and not with nature or man. Genesis 1:1 says, "In the beginning *God* created the heavens and the earth" (emphasis added). God is the first and the last. He is before the beginning and after the end of human history. His existence and presence give our lives meaning. We don't manufacture meaning via our own efforts.

The narrative continues with Genesis 1:26–28:

Then God said, "Let us make man in our image, after our likeness. And let them have dominion over the fish of the sea and over the birds of the heavens and over the livestock and over all the earth and over every creeping thing that creeps on the earth."

So God created man in his own image,
in the image of God he created him;
male and female he created them.

And God blessed them. And God said to them, "Be fruitful and multiply and fill the earth and subdue it and have dominion over the fish of the sea and over the birds of the heavens and over every living thing that moves on the earth."

Identity and Purpose

Note our identity, made male and female in the image of God, and our purpose, to be fruitful and to have dominion over everything on the earth in God's stead. Our identity and purpose are intimately related. We find in the biblical narrative that being made in the image of God means that we are reasonable and volitional creatures, with the freedom to live in the midst of reality and to extend His rule as His representatives.

As the Bible Project says, "In the beginning of the Bible, we see God as the all-powerful creator and king of the earth. As the king and the creator, He has authority over creation. One of the first things He does, though, is to create mankind and give them all authority to rule over creation by making them in His image."[1]

Theologians call this purpose of extending God's rule by His image-bearers the cultural mandate. That mandate has two subordinating principles—first, a social mandate to form families; second, a developmental mandate to be stewards over creation. As the Bible Project says, "The image of God in the Bible that we are given shows that ruling over the earth means to cultivate it, harnessing its raw potential and moving creation forward."[2]

Stewarding creation includes but is not limited to agricultural pursuits such as farming and forestry. It includes *all* the arts and sciences, politics, and every field of human endeavor. Human beings, male and female and made in the *Imago Dei* (the "image of God"), are called to unlock all the secrets of God's creation for God's glory . . . , human good and the flourishing of creation. Christians, who acknowledge the deity to Jesus Christ, are to focus their lifework on glorifying Him and advancing His kingdom. As the Dutch statesman Abraham Kuyper stated, "[T]here is not a square inch in the whole domain of our human existence over which Christ, who is Sovereign over all, does not cry: 'Mine!'"[3]

The Quest for Truth

This Jesus Christ, whom Christians worship as God, stated unequivocally, "I am the way, and the truth, and the life" (John 14:6), and so His followers are unalterably committed to knowing and living the truth. Another key statement about truth that will guide us in our pursuit of education is found in John 8:31–32:

> So Jesus said to the Jews who had believed him, "If you abide in my word, you are truly my disciples, and you will know the truth, and the truth will set you free."

In this short passage several points bear directly on our quest for the truth and on our calling to claim every domain of human existence—including education—for Him.

Note, first, that Jesus is addressing "the Jews who had believed him." These were "believers" but not yet "disciples." Simple acknowledgment of Jesus without heart change and a life to match is not enough.

Second, Jesus is making a distinction between believers and disciples. To be a disciple is to abide in God's Word. The word *abide* translates the Greek word μένω (*menō*), which has the active, life-giving, organic sense of "stay," "wait for," "continue to exist," and "keep on." We are called to *truly* be His disciples . . . by abiding in His Word. That is, we are to cherish it, study it, walk by it, and share it. It is to transform us and our lives.

Third, there are good consequences for continuing in God's Word. When we continue living in God's Word, we will "know the truth." The truth, which conforms to reality, can be *known*. Think of the difference this makes!

Fourth, knowing the truth leads to freedom. No longer must we grope forever in the dark seeking vainly for progress, peace, health, and life. Lives and cultures founded on the truth will flourish, because they have been designed to flourish. There is an organic relationship between truth and freedom. The truth will set us free. And, conversely, there are negative consequences to believing lies: bondage and poverty.[4]

Our Response

A second short Bible passage about truth to consider is Acts 17:11: "Now [the Berean] Jews were more noble than those in Thessalonica; they received the word with all eagerness, examining the Scriptures daily to see if [the things Paul said] were so."

The preaching of the good news about Jesus's life, death, and resurrection called for a response in the Roman Empire of the first century—as it does in our day. That response is not to be based on how the gospel makes us *feel* but on whether it is *true*—whether it corresponds to reality.

Note that we are told that the Bereans were nobler than the Thessalonians. The Greek word translated "more noble" is εὐγενῆς (*eugenēs*) and means to be *open-minded*. Think of this as a contrast to the closed-minded person. The mind that is open to new ideas, quick to ask questions in search of the truth, is nobler than a mind that accepts assumptions without questioning. Why? Because truth is of paramount importance, and its pursuit is a noble profession. As historian Michael Leeden put it, "We need to restore the tradition of rebellious nonconformity."[5]

The Bereans were interested in *truth*. Where was truth to be found? Truth is found in the Scriptures. Yes, there are other sources of truth in God's world, but only the Scriptures are *completely trustworthy* in the affirmations they make about God, the universe, and our place in it. As Jesus said to His Father in heaven, "Your word is truth" (John 17:17). It is this word that tells us truly, "In the beginning God created the heavens and the earth."

Note as well that the Bereans examined the Scriptures *every day* to check the veracity of Paul's words. They *abided* in the Scriptures. They wanted to discover whether the apostle Paul was telling them the truth about Jesus (Acts 17:11). How would they know? They searched the Scriptures. Their response is a model for all of us who claim to follow Jesus and who seek the truth.

The Bereans knew something critical that we would do well to remember: Truth is *revealed* through the Word of God. As Jesus prayed in John 17:17: "Sanctify them in the truth; your word is truth." The Word of God, the Scriptures of the Old and New Testaments, constitutes what theologians have called God's special revelation. God revealed this body of truth to human beings because we never could have discovered it by ourselves. But that is not the end of the matter.

SG-1b Hidden and Discovered

Truth is also *hidden* in order to be discovered. In Proverbs 25:2 we read these wonderfully playful words: "It is the glory of God to conceal things, but the glory of kings is to search things out." In this divine game of hide and seek, God conceals things so that we may "search things out." The Hebrew word is חָקַר (*ḥā·qăr*), and it means to "explore, search out, discover, probe, sound out, examine, test . . ."[6]

We find the same concept in Psalm 111:2–3, where the psalmist says that God's works in creation are great, full of splendor and majesty, so much so that those who delight in them, study them.

Here we find the fount of science. God has hidden things about Himself and creation that He expects humankind to search out and discover. Here is the home of the inquisitive mind of the explorer, the adventurer, the detective, the tinkerer, the scientist. What a profound and beautiful picture of the playful God leaving clues of hidden treasure for His children to discover, riddles for them to solve.

So, truth is revealed through the Word of God and discovered, for example, in math and science, physics and astronomy—through the works of God. As we have seen, human beings were placed here to govern creation (Genesis 1:26–29; 2:15, 19–20; Psalm 8:3–6; 115:16). It is important to study, search, and discover the things hidden by God in order to properly fulfill the cultural mandate to govern the earth.

God's Clues

God provides us with plenty of clues for our God-given task to search things out and take care of His creation. The sun, moon, and stars were given to help us. Genesis 1:14 says, "And God said, 'Let there be lights in the expanse of the heavens to separate the day from the night. And let them be for signs and for seasons, and for days and years.'"

The psalmist David understood that God's creation *communicates* real knowledge of God and His work.

> The heavens *declare* the glory of God,
>   and the sky above *proclaims* his handiwork.
> Day to day pours out *speech*,
>   and night to night *reveals* knowledge.
> There is no *speech*, nor are there words,
>   whose *voice* is not heard.
> Their *voice* goes out through all the earth,
>   and their *words* to the end of the world. (Psalm 19:1–4a, emphasis added)

Note all the verbs of communication in this text, and all that is revealed. The atheists claim that the universe is silent. The atheists are wrong. God exists and is not silent. God speaks to us, not only supernaturally through His Word, but also "naturally," through His creation. The great Protestant Reformers Martin Luther and John Calvin spoke of two books: God's Word and His works. Theologians call these two books special revelation and general revelation. Even scientists find themselves strangely attracted.

No less a scientist and atheist than Nobel laureate Jacques Monod has written in his book *Chance and Necessity*:

> Objectivity nevertheless obliges us to recognize the teleonomic character of living organisms, to admit that in their structure and performance they act projectively—realize and pursue a purpose. Here therefore, at least in appearance, lies a profound epistemological contradiction. In fact the central problem of biology lies with this very contradiction, which, if it is only apparent, must be resolved; or else proven to be utterly insoluble, if that should turn out indeed to be the case.[7]

Monod acknowledges that objectivity requires the scientist to recognize that the structure and performance of living things reveals purposeful design. Their structure, in other words, reveals their Creator, who designed them for a purpose.

This raises a problem for naturalistic scientists who deny the existence of a God. How does Monod handle this? He calls this dilemma a "profound metaphysical contradiction." What scientists have discovered does not comport with their modern atheistic assumptions. These assumptions cannot be reconciled to their observations without acknowledging a personal Designer.

This is exactly the argument that the apostle Paul makes in Romans 1:19–20 (NKJV):

> . . . because what may be known of God is *manifest in them*, for God has shown it to them. For since the creation of the world *His invisible attributes are clearly seen*, being understood by the things that are made, *even His eternal power and Godhead, so that they are without excuse* (emphasis added).

Monod acknowledges the clarity of God's general revelation; therefore, the logic of his position *should* compel him to bow in worship. Why is that?

Paul says that all human beings can know (1) that God exists, and (2) something about His nature through the things that He has made. This general revelation through creation is so utterly clear that there is no excuse for anyone to deny God's existence.

The Three Books

Note that Paul says that God's works reveal His existence and something of His character. Paul argues that His works reveal truth about God in two ways: (1) inside humans ("manifest in them") and (2) outside them ("by the things that are made").

- First, He has revealed Himself *inside of human beings* by making us in His image. We as human beings have the ability to reason (an attribute of intellect), we have a will (the attribute of purpose), and we have a heart (the attribute of moral responsibility).
- Second, He has revealed himself *outside of humanity* in the rest of creation. This revelation extends from the appearance of the quark in the deepest recesses of inner space to the farthest-flung edges of the universe in the unimaginably distant reaches of outer space. These two forms of general revelation were recognized by early educational reformers and scientists, who spoke of a *tripartite view* of God's revelation. Its component parts include:

> The book of *revelation*—special revelation—the Bible
> The book of *reality*—nature—science (a la Aristotle)
> The book of *reason*—or logic—philosophy (a la Plato)

Scientists who backed this approach included sons of the Reformation who spent their lives studying the works of God, tethered to the Word of God. As theists, they affirmed an integrated view of the universe, with no separation between the Word of God and the works of God.

- Galileo (1564–1642) was an Italian polymath-scientist who stood at the transition of natural philosophy, that is, theistic science, and modern atheistic science. He studied both God's Word and His works. He confirmed that the earth and the planets revolved around the sun.
- Francis Bacon (1561–1627), English philosopher, scientist, and politician, has been called the father of modern science for his emphasis

on careful observation of God's works. He used inductive reasoning to draw conclusions from observations. Bacon wrote, "Knowledge is the rich storehouse for the glory of the Creator and the relief of man's estate."[8]

- Isaac Newton (1642–1727), English mathematician, astronomer, theologian, author, and physicist, is one of the most influential scientists of all time. Newton was a key figure in the scientific revolution. Like other theistic scientists of the day, he recognized that God has revealed Himself in creation. Newton wrote, "Plato is my friend, Aristotle is my friend, but my greatest friend is truth."[9]

This impulse to study God's works in creation led earlier Christian scientists to found research universities and the oldest national scientific institution in the world, the Royal Society in England. The society was established in 1660, largely by scientists who understood that human beings are meant to discover what God has hidden in creation. (Newton was an early member.) They believed that these discoveries would enable humankind to govern creation. Indeed, we see how science and technology help us fight the curses of natural evil in the world, such as floods, droughts, famine, earthquakes, tsunamis, and tornados, as well as the various diseases and illnesses, like the current Covid-19 virus ravaging the world today, that mark the human condition.

Educational Reformers

Such scientists who sought to discover hidden truths in God's creation for the benefit of humankind were paralleled by reformers in education, especially three prominent theologians:

- John Amos Comenius (1592–1670), a Czech Moravian, rather than John Dewey, is known by many as the father of modern education.[10]
- William Ames (1576–1633), an English Puritan, wrote of *encyclopedia* (the circle of knowledge) and of the Six Arts—that is, an integrative, comprehensive form of education with God at the center.[11]
- Johann Heinrich Alsted (1588–1638), a prolific German theologian, was known as "the true parent of all the Encyclopædias."[12]

These educational trailblazers, all from the Reformed and Puritan tradition, knew that truth is found at the intersection of the three books—Scripture, nature, and reason. The three books were foundational in the creation of Western civilization and stood at the forefront of North American education. As Comenius said,

"The only true, genuine and plain way of Philosophy is to fetch all things from sense, reason and Scripture."

Historian David Scott points out that "Comenius went on to say that the end of scholarly endeavor is not to merely add to the wood pile of human knowledge, but to grow a living tree that from its roots to its boughs and fruit reflects the image of the words and works of its divine Creator."[13]

Veritas

SG-1c

Comenius laid the foundations for an educational system that built a nation. Comenius wrote the *Didactica Magna* (*The Whole Art of Teaching*), in which he articulated biblical concepts of a unified field of knowledge (everything must be taught) and universal education (to everyone). In his *A Reformation of Schooles*, Comenius cast the vision for an educational philosophy that encompassed mind and heart, Word and world:

> And Praised be thou, O Lord, forever, which dost likewise give us thy works and word for a pattern, whereby to erect this . . . temple of Wisdom: that as thy word and works are true and lively representations of thee: so this, which we are about, may prove a true, and lively image of thy word and works.[14]

Comenius understood that "we [humans] are about" the business of erecting a "temple of Wisdom," i.e., creating culture to the glory of God. He knew that God, through His works and His Word, has revealed Himself as the primary Creator, who spoke into being the world. In studying the creation and the Book, we discover God's nature and the nature of reality—*veritas*, or truth. We are then to mimic God by building our cultures (secondary worlds) to reflect God and His primary world. As we do, we fill the earth with His glory and become wise. Education is a key means toward this all-encompassing end.

The Puritan vision can be expressed as in the chart below:

THE REFORMERS' VISION BECOMES THE PURITAN VISION

Veritas
The Pursuit of Truth

Encyclopedia
The Circle of Knowledge

Eupraxia
The Practice of Right Living

Following the approach of Comenius, American universities originally existed so that students and faculty could pursue and practice truth for the glory of God. These institutions of higher learning instilled in their students not only knowledge but understanding (the meaning of what they know) and wisdom (the moral practice of truth). The outcome was a land of freedom and opportunity, a nation founded on an idea—freedom, which attracted immigrants from all over the world.

It was largely the Puritans who founded higher education in colonial North America. Colleges such as Harvard (founded 1636), Yale (1701), Princeton (1746), Rutgers (1766), and Dartmouth (1769) were among those built on their Reformation educational philosophy, known as *technologia*. This vision, what might be rightly called a Biblical theology of education, has three parts:

1. Veritas
2. Encyclopedia
3. Eupraxia

In the next three sections, we shall discuss each of these in turn. First, we will consider the first aspect of the Puritan theology of education, *veritas*—the pursuit of truth.

The Harvard Shield

Eight years after landing in New England, the Puritan fathers established Harvard College (now Harvard University) to educate pastors and civic leaders. On

December 27, 1643, the Board of Overseers of Harvard College declared that "there shall be a Colledge seale in forme following."

The first conceptual draft of the Harvard shield showed the three books and the word *veritas*—Latin for *truth*. Evidently the drawing was filed away and rediscovered 200 years later at the time of the bicentennial celebration of Harvard. In 1843, then Harvard President Josiah Quincy revealed the sketch. The Harvard Corporation made it the official pattern for all subsequent renditions of the shields. In 1692, the motto adopted by the university was *Veritas Christo et Ecclesiae*, "Truth for Christ and the Church."[15]

HARVARD'S ORIGINAL SHIELD: THE THREE BOOKS

- **The book of revelation -** *Special Revelation – The Bible*
- **The book of creation -** ***Reality*** – through the senses – *Aristotle*
- **The book of the mind -** ***Reason*** or Logic – *Plato*

- ***Veritas*** **— Truth is found at the intersection of the "books" of Scripture, creation, and reason.**

Anyone walking around the campus of this Ivy League school could find evidence of this commitment to *veritas*. The photograph below, for example, taken at Harvard, shows the "ve-ri-tas" inscribed across three books.

iStock.com/RiverNorthPhotography

We have seen these three books before,[16] but why is the bottom one face down? Georgia Purdom observes, "Interestingly, the top two books on the shield are face up while the bottom book is face down. Some have argued that this symbolizes the limits of reason, and the need for God's revelation."[17]

To use an analogy from C.S. Lewis, it is the sun that gives light to the world and everything in it, so it is the book of the Bible that gives light to the other two books, reason and reality.

As Purdom notes, the current version of Harvard's motto represents a significant spiritual erosion. The single word "veritas" remains, but the original slogan, *Christo et Ecclesiae* ("for Christ and the Church"), is conspicuously absent. The modern seal also displays three books that are open, but the facedown book has been turned over to match the others: there are no limits to human reason or science now!

This is just one example, but it clearly illustrates that today's American culture is atheistic to the core. History is being rewritten—deconstructed, actually. Ignoring history, modern secularists now argue that Western societies are rooted exclusively in the European Enlightenment and not in the Judeo-Christian framework.

Harvard's first mission statement was explicitly Christ-centered:

> Let every student be plainly instructed, and earnestly pressed to consider well, the main end of his life and studies is, to know God and Jesus Christ which is eternal life, John 17.3 and therefore to lay Christ in the bottom, as the only foundation of all sound knowledge and learning.[18]

Christ is the focus of all of life and vocation. It was this conviction that laid the groundwork for Christian culture and self-government. Sadly, the Western world no longer operates from a biblical worldview. But it is only the biblical worldview that provides a foundation for free, just, prosperous, and compassionate nations, because all truth is God's truth. There is one God and one reality, which is created and fulfills His design. Thus, truth is comprehensive (with no dichotomy between the so-called sacred and the secular) and integrative (providing a unified field of knowledge).

The Biblical Worldview Abandoned

With the rise of the Enlightenment in Europe and Darwinian science in the West, the biblical worldview was abandoned for secularism (the belief that religion should be excluded from everyday life as unimportant) or atheism (the belief that God does not exist). As the West became increasingly secularized, most people, along with many Christians, turned from the biblical worldview, leading to our *post-moral* culture of pragmatism and cultural relativism.

Rather than engaging with atheism on the playing field of ideas, Christians adopted the ancient Greek dualistic worldview, along with its belief in a sacred-secular divide. These in turn produced an evangelical gnosticism, which separated the spiritual from the secular, and faith from reason.

Something similar is happening with the current materialist philosophy that has prevailed since the Enlightenment. It is dying, because people are looking for something that recognizes the spiritual dimension of human life. But the modern Western church's gnostic surrender keeps it from offering a comprehensive answer to life's basic questions. Western culture therefore is drifting into neopaganism, or postmodern animism.

This can be illustrated with the use of the Harvard shield as a metaphorical example. First there was the elimination of the banner "For Christ and the Church." Then, as evolutionism took over the point of integration for all society, the Bible, the book of special revelation, was removed. Moderns left the world without spirit and in what could be called a post-moral state. This left the books of reason and reality. The Darwinian faith assumed that human beings could understand all there is to understand through philosophy and science.

WEAKENING PURSUIT OF TRUTH
ELIMINATED ONE BOOK

The Moderns

- Got rid of the banner for Christ and the Church
- Removed the book of **Revelation**
- Kept the books of Reason and Reality

The Modern Shield

But as the modern world with its emphasis on material things began to shrivel the soul, people began to turn to the "spiritual" and more mystical realm for answers. The postmodern world has thrown out the books of reason and reality. We now live in a post-truth culture, as illustrated by this diagram:

END OF THE PURSUIT OF TRUTH

THE POSTMODERNS ELIMINATE THE THREE BOOKS

The Postmoderns

- Went further than the moderns
- Eliminated the other two books:
  - **Reason**
  - **Reality**

The Postmodern Shield

All that we see unfolding in the world today can be rooted in the loss of the three books, revelation, reason and reality, so wonderfully represented in the Harvard Shield.

Combining Reason and Revelation

REASON AND REVELATION

REASON

	REVELATION	NO REVELATION
REASON	• **VERITAS** • "Orthodox" Christians • Jews • (Reformed) Muslims	• **RATIONALISM** • Atheism • Pagan Humanism • Evolutionism
NO REASON	• **FIDEISM** • Many Evangelical and Charismatic Christians • Fundamentalist Muslims • Some traditional religions	• **IRRATIONALISM** • Pagan Animism • Postmodernism • New Age • Neo-Paganism

NO REASON

Every culture, and every worldview, has a different way of looking at, and combining, two critical ways of knowing and interacting with the universe—that is, what is *true*. Those areas are reason—what we can learn from our own efforts as human beings—and revelation—what we can learn from God's communication to us via His Word. Biblical theism, along with both atheistic and postmodern worldviews, each combines reason and revelation in fundamentally different ways. This summary will help us see the differences, and why they matter so much.

- **Revelation and Reason.** Biblical theism acknowledges that reason (from our being made in God's image) and revelation (from God's Word) lie at the heart of *veritas*. Biblical theism holds that a unified field of knowledge exists that is binding on all people. Truth is objective. *Veritas* is what brings freedom and economic prosperity to nations. This is the framework of orthodox Christianity and believed by the early church, various church fathers (Augustine and Aquinas), the Reformers (fourteenth to sixteenth centuries), and their Puritan successors. This worldview gave rise to modern science and paved the way for the founding of the United States. As Vishal Mangalwadi has said, orthodox Christianity established "[r]esearch universities and labs . . . built on the knowledge that God's words and works conceal matters, [and] we are endowed with reason in order to discover hidden treasures."[19]
- **Reason without Revelation.** Tragically, biblical theism gave way to rationalism—reason without revelation. This was the paradigm of both the deistic Enlightenment (seventeenth to eighteenth centuries) and modern atheism (nineteenth to twentieth centuries), the belief that all knowledge begins and ends with man. It was promoted by Kant, Voltaire, Rousseau, and Hume and provided the framework for the French Revolution. Darwin's theory of evolution made life without the Creator seem plausible. Reason without revelation became the framework. Truth, morals, and beauty became relative. The *creation* was reduced to mere *nature*, voiding the universe of transcendence, putting man in the small box of a naturalistic and mechanistic universe. Mainline Protestantism was born by adapting Christianity to this framework.
- **Revelation without Reason.** As rationalism spread and segments of the church adopted it, certain Christian leaders sought to remain faithful to core, orthodox teaching, identifying themselves as fundamentalists. But instead of defending the biblical worldview that establishes orthodoxy, they abandoned Christianity's foundations to opt instead for the sa-

cred-secular dichotomy of the ancient Greeks. This movement brought in evangelical gnosticism, which began in the late nineteenth century and remains in force today.

This is a move to fideism—revelation without reason. Its bitter fruit included sub-Christian strains of anti-intellectualism and super spirituality that led to the disastrous abandonment of reason for faith alone by large sections of the church. The university, where all of God's creation is explored, was replaced with the Bible school, which reduced the proper scope of study to Scripture and spiritual things.

Now, there is absolutely *nothing* wrong with the rigorous study of the Bible from an orthodox perspective. In fact, a proper understanding of God's Word written is the sine qua non of all true learning. But rejecting the truth we are able to discover via reason and the created order eventually led to an abandonment of the culture. Without *veritas*, the church became orthodox in name only.

Ironically, this framework of faith without reason has positioned the twenty-first-century church to blend right in with our postmodern, post-truth culture. Most Christians today regard the spiritual as the only realm of importance. Things secular are deemed "worldly," of inferior value to things sacred. This heresy is opposed to the biblical view, which recognizes that spiritual and secular are different yet equally important.

- **Neither Reason nor Revelation.** As people grapple with their place in a supposedly soulless world, they are beginning to reevaluate what they believe, because rationalism cannot satisfy the deepest longings of our hearts. The tragic mimicking of the world by mainline denominations and the unnecessary evangelical lurch into culture-abandoning gnosticism have created a vacuum that waits to be filled. Sadly, because of our abdication, the West is now turning to irrationalism, replacing both revelation and reason with solace. Rooted in the animistic worship of creation, this form of neopaganism does not seek truth, believing there is no such thing. It seeks instead a feeling of personal well-being. God is conceived of as one undivided spirit. We search now only for the "god within you." This framework, which has given birth to the gender identity movement, is erasing the concept of transcendent masculine and feminine, as well as the biological reality of male and female.

Today the church is responding to the rise of postmodernism with a new dichotomy. The flourishing anti-intellectualism and hyper-spirituality found in the church today deny reason and reality. The new dichotomy following them holds that love is more important than truth. Such "love" knows nothing of "speaking the truth in love" (Ephesians 4:15). Instead, it celebrates what God condemns in His Word.

For example, Pete Buttigieg, the Democratic mayor of South Bend, is in a homosexual relationship that the government counts as a marriage. At a political fundraiser, Buttigieg said, "[It] has made me a better man [and] . . . moved me closer to God. If being gay was a choice, it was a choice that was made far above my pay grade."[20] Of course, Scripture explicitly condemns this,[21] but Buttigieg can suggest with a straight face that it is good for him, and even that it was God's idea, because of the love-truth divide in which feelings trump all. SG-1d

Drifting into Danger

The rise of Darwinism caused many in the West to abandon the biblical worldview and to order their daily affairs as though God did not exist. Today's church faces a similar danger. We are drifting into a postmodern worldview that abandons reason and reality and encourages us to live by our emotions alone. The abandonment of the truth-love comprehensive nature of the scripture and manifest in the cross, leaves the church with a love/truth dichotomy, with love taking precedence over truth, culminating in what is being called the "woke-church."

The Puritans, imperfect inheritors of Christian orthodoxy, were what Dr. Leland Ryken called *worldly saints*,[22] in the best sense of the term. They pursued truth, *veritas*. They understood it to be comprehensive and integrative, with no separation of nature from grace, nor science from theology, nor work from worship. Unlike much of the church in our era, they reasoned from the moral and metaphysical grand narrative of Scripture. We must learn to do the same as we come to understand and apply the organizing principle of a virtuous life.

The Puritans, as I have said, called this principle *technologia*. The word is derived from the Latin words *techno* ("skill" or "art") and *logia* ("the study of"). It means "the study of the integration of all the arts and science." It is not to be confused with the modern concept of technology—applied science, or technique. Technology and technique deal strictly with the practical question, "Can we do it?" They raise no moral question, such as, "Should we do it?"

In Puritan usage, *technologia* was a Latin transliteration of a Greek word meaning "an applied system relating all knowledge and its proper use in life." To say it a little differently, *technologia* is the organizing principle for a virtuous life, a life of purpose, connecting all of life to the advancement of the kingdom of God. It covers every good thing in this world, leading to what the Puritans called *encyclopedia*—the circle of knowledge. It is this second aspect of the Puritan theology of education we will examine now.

Encyclopedia

The rise of atheism in the West undermined not only widespread belief in God but the existing consensus about absolute truth and morality. When society surrendered an infinite and transcendent reference point for all of life, mere individuals become the center of the universe. Moral and metaphysical relativism became the framework for people's life and work.

The resulting changes in higher education have been profound. The word *university* is derived from *universus*, which is formed from two words—*uni* (one) and *versus* (turned)—thus "turned into one." The concept was one of unity and diversity, a unity of diverse fields of study.

But now universities simply have diversities, with no true unity. The university is no longer seen as a *community* of diverse scholars. Instead, students and professors work and study in silos, learning "more and more about less and less." Every area of knowledge has been cut off from all the rest. Instead, specialization in a pluralistic world has become the norm. The only unifying principle today is evolutionary ideology.

This shift has produced great fragmentation in all of life. Rather than seeing ourselves in relationship to our Creator, our fellow human beings, and the rest of creation, we view ourselves as isolated, autonomous beings in a silent universe. This is the loneliness of modern men and women.

Contrast this unhappy trajectory with the Puritan concept of *technologia*. This philosophy of education includes not only the pursuit of *veritas* but also posits an integrated and comprehensive understanding of knowledge, based on the reality of God's transcendence (His existence outside the universe). In his *Vision of Veritas*, David Scott writes, "*Technologia* was the skill of harmonizing all of these resulting academic disciplines in a circle of knowledge, called 'encyclopedia.'"[23]

The term "circle of knowledge" was first used in the 1530s to mean "course of instruction." Its literal definition is "training in a circle," i.e., the "circle" of arts and sciences. It is derived from two Greek words—*enkyklios*, "circular," and *paideia*, "education, child-rearing." This understanding of "encyclopedia" has been seen, not coincidentally, as the indispensable basis of a "liberal education."

Ames, the Puritan educational reformer, also described this approach to education as a circle of knowledge, stating, "The comprehension of all those arts by which things emanate from the Ens Primum [First Being] and return again *to* him is called Encyclopedia, whose first link of the circular chain is logic and the last theology."[24]

Such thinking is largely a lost art among Christians today. As Francis Schaeffer wrote in *A Christian Manifesto*, "The basic problem of the Christians . . . is that they have seen things in bits and pieces instead of totals."[25]

By contrast, the diagram below[26] illustrates how we can see education as a unified circle of knowledge:

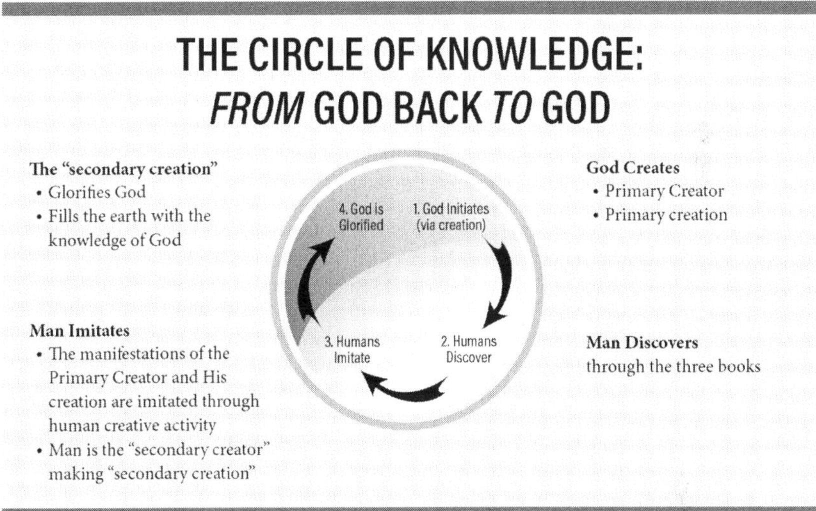

The framework begins with God, the *Primary Creator*. Man, made in the *imago Dei*, has the ability to *discover* the Creator and the created order. He does so through the three books: Scripture, reason, and nature (what is more properly called "creation"). From these three sources human beings learn about God, who is the Primary Creator, and the primary creation, which is commonly called nature.

Then, through his own imagination and creative activity, man *imitates* what he has discovered. In so doing, he is a co-creator with God, building from the foundations and principles He has established. Man's secondary creation is not more nature but culture. Scott summarizes: "Through scholarship, humankind discovers God's design and forms this knowledge into an imitation of God's design in the disciplines of the arts and sciences."[27]

Man, in his calling as the secondary creator, reveals the primary Creator and His creation. As man creates culture, God is *glorified* and the earth is *filled with the knowledge of God*.

But the circle does not end here. Indeed, it goes on through all eternity. When Jesus teaches His disciples to pray to the Father "your kingdom come, your will be done, on earth as it is in heaven" (Matthew 6:10), He is telling us to participate in God's bringing the heavenly kingdom *down to earth.* C. S. Lewis called this process transposition.[28]

This is the Great Commission of the church—making disciples of all nations, baptizing them, and teaching them to do all that Christ has commanded (Matthew 28:18–20) during this time between Christ's resurrection and His return at the end of history. Jesus wants the perfect kingdom of heaven to be expanded *on earth as it is in heaven,*[29] and therefore He commands His followers to *disciple all nations.* Through obedience to God's ordinances, the first fruits[30] of heaven are manifested in our broken nations. Something from heaven is to be transposed to earth. This is the task given to God's people.

This task is intimately connected to the prior creation mandate to be fruitful and have dominion over the earth (Genesis 1:26–28). Nothing that has glorified God in this world will end here. In perfect glory it will be *transposed to heaven* to adorn the City of God.

> And the city has no need of sun or moon to shine on it, for the glory of God gives it light, and its lamp is the Lamb. By its light will the nations walk, and the kings of the earth will bring their glory into it, and its gates will never be shut by day—and there will be no night there. They will bring into it the glory and the honor of the nations. But nothing unclean will ever enter it, nor anyone who does what is detestable or false, but only those who are written in the Lamb's book of life. (Revelation 21:23–27)

God is on a mission and has called us to join Him. Two mandates describe our mission: the First Commission—the cultural mandate given at creation, and the Second Commission—aka, the Great Commission to disciple nations, given at the risen Christ's coronation. These twin commissions provide a unified field of knowledge, an integrative principle, for all education.

This circle of creation, discovery, imitation, and glory is the circle of knowledge. The Puritans were interested not only in *knowing* the truth; like the Jews, they wanted to *do* the truth. They understood the indivisible bond between knowing and doing. Their term for this correlation between knowing and doing was *eupraxia*, which we will consider more fully in the next section.

We see evidence for the circle in the Bible. In John's Revelation, Christ states, "I am the Alpha and the Omega, the beginning and the end" (21:6). In a similar vein, the apostle Paul declares the supremacy of Christ:

> For by him all things were created, in heaven and on earth, visible and invisible, whether thrones or dominions or rulers or authorities—all things were created through him or for him. And he is before all things, and in him all things hold together. And he is the head of the body, the church. He is the beginning, the firstborn from the dead, that in everything he might be preeminent. (Colossians 1:16–18)

Scripture shows that Christ is both the center and the end of encyclopedia. He is the ontological Creator of all things, and all things will find their purpose in the eschatological consummation when He returns. In that day the godly fruits of man's secondary creation will fully glorify God.

Let's dig a little deeper to see how the circle of knowledge works in specific areas of education.[31] Ames held that there are six "arts":

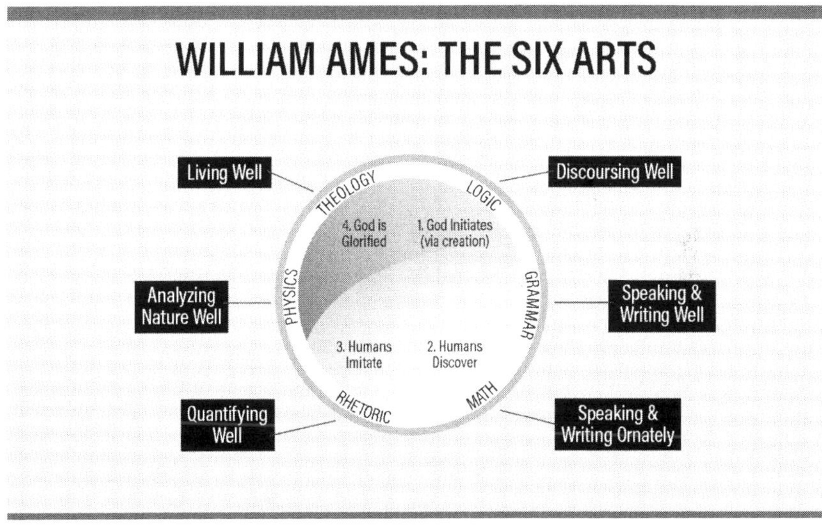

- Logic: The Art of Discoursing Well
- Grammar: The Art of Speaking and Writing Well
- Rhetoric: The Art of Speaking and Writing Ornately
- Math: The Art of Qualifying Well
- Physics: The Art of Analyzing Nature Well
- Theology: The Art of Living Well

In the Puritan vision, the six arts and the circle of knowledge are the foundation for all education. They prepare people for their life and work. In this framework, *vocation is not separated from theological reflection, but founded upon it.*

Scott writes:

> [S]cholarship itself is only one of the many vocations. Each vocation is a faculty or applied use of one or more of these disciplines. Because humankind was created in the image of the Divine Artist, the vocations allow the human being to participate in the ongoing divine master plan of creation. Vocation functions spiritually as a kind of performance art—a participation in God's ongoing mission for creation. The human being as an artisan can follow in the footsteps of the Divine Artist.[32]

Technologia thus is a wholistic (see discussion in Chapter Five, page 97, of the unique spelling of this word [generally "holistic"] used throughout this book) curriculum that relates work to worldview and first principles as articulated in the Scriptures. Its systematic, well-defined, and comprehensive framework helps each individual to "glorify God, and enjoy Him forever."[33] It provides the framework for men and women to understand and pursue their own unique, God-given callings. Seen in this way, *technologia* becomes the moral and metaphysical "map in the mind" that leads to one's lifework, and the practice of what is true, good, and beautiful.

What does this kind of life look like? Now, we turn to the third part of the
SG-1f Puritan theology of education.

Eupraxia

The end of real education, in the concept of *technologia*, is *eupraxia*, the practice of right living. This is the connection between knowing and doing.

Noah Webster (1758–1843) was a descendant of Governor William Bradford of Plymouth Colony. Webster observed the rise of atheism in Europe. While the French Revolution sought to establish a society free *from* religion, the American Revolution provided for freedom *of* religion.[34] This truth would have profound implications for education.

Webster came to faith in Christ later in life, and from 1808 until 1828 he labored to define the words that would build a nation. Webster's *Blue-Backed Speller* taught five generations of children how to read. Capturing the language of liberty and the new Constitution, Webster's 1828 *Dictionary* was built from the foundation for a biblical worldview. More than that, it preserved the biblical meanings of words as they were used in the world's first constitutional republic.

As we have seen, Christ and the Bible were at the center of the Puritan vision for education. Webster made the same connection, saying, "Education is useless without the Bible."[35] Max Weber, the eminent twentieth-century sociologist whose study of the Reformation's liberating economic impact gave us the phrase "the Protestant work ethic," also noted the transforming power of words. Historian Niall Ferguson says,

> Protestantism made the West not only work, but also save and read. The Industrial Revolution . . . also required an increase in the intensity and duration of work, combined with the accumulation of capital through saving and investment. Above all, it depended on the accumulation of human capital. The literacy that Protestantism promoted was vital to all of this. On reflection, we would do better to talk about the Protestant word ethic.[36]

The European Reformers wanted to reform all of life, as captured by their Latin motto *Reformatio Vitae*. To accomplish this grand vision, they needed a comprehensive framework, what became known as *technologia*. John Calvin, the French theologian, pastor, and Reformer in Geneva, believed that the church had been entrusted with the primary teaching role for the entire society. In fact, the light in Geneva spread throughout Europe, from Cranmer and Knox in the British Isles to Vermigli in Italy. Even the communist state of Belarus has recognized the Reformer Francis Skaryna (1486–1551) as the father of the country.[37] The church was to help shape the conscience of the nation.

The Reformers, in fact, saw the church as the primary agent for social transformation. The church's purpose was to disciple not only individuals but *cultures* by teaching the cities and the nations to obey all that Christ commands (Matthew 28:18–20).

Youmans writes:

> Pastors were the key influencers of this era. They were the educators in the communities. They taught young boys during the week and their sermons, which often lasted several hours on Sundays, taught the adults. In the colonial era, pastors' sermons were passed through the congregation and fathers would

> dissect the sermon at night around the fire with his wife and children. He would re-teach the principles contained in them and help his children learn how to reason with truth and apply it to their own lives. The sermons of this era . . . were used mightily by God to educate several generations, who are now said to be the most literate of any generation in history. The Bible for the Calvinists was their primer of education and their political textbook.[38]

Discipleship during the Reformation was not limited, as it often is today, to spiritual exercises—teaching believers to pray, read the Word, worship, fellowship, and evangelize. These are vitally necessary, of course, but not sufficient for truly reforming a society.

The Reformers in Geneva understood the church's teaching role in society—to fill the city and the earth with the knowledge of God. Calvin and his associates studied the Scriptures to see their application to society. New converts were taught the implications of their faith in all areas of life. The church was called to contribute to the building of the city or the nation from biblical worldview foundations, helping to bring a moral and metaphysical vision to the nation. Pastors and civic leaders came from all over Europe to see the Geneva "laboratory," a city seeking to apply biblical patterns to all of life.[39]

The Reformers in Geneva took the words of Christ seriously. Geneva became known as the Protestant Rome and "the City Set on a Hill," reflecting Christ's words in the Sermon on the Mount:

> You are the light of the world. A city set on a hill cannot be hidden. Nor do people light a lamp and put it under a basket, but on a stand, and it gives light to all in the house. In the same way, let your light shine before others, so that they may see your good works and give glory to your Father who is in heaven. (Matthew 5:14–16)

Geneva became a light for Europe and for what would become the United States. The light spread from John Calvin's (1509–1564) Geneva to John Knox's (1514–1572) Scotland to Puritan England (1660s) and finally to Puritan "New England" (1620–1680). The First Great Awakening (1734–1750) of Jonathan Edwards led to the founding of the new nation—the United States of America.

The concept of Geneva's City on the Hill came to America through a wealthy English Puritan lawyer, John Winthrop (1587/8–1649). Winthrop was the CEO of a venture capital corporation, the Massachusetts Bay Colony, and a twelve-term governor of Boston. While on the ship *Arabella*, on his way to the new world, Winthrop preached the sermon "A Model of Charity." In it he stated,

> For we must consider that we shall be as a city upon a hill. The eyes of all people are upon us. So that if we shall deal falsely with our God in this work we have undertaken, and so cause him to withdraw his present help from us, we shall be a story and a by-word through the world. We shall open the mouths of enemies to speak evil of the ways of God.[40]

David Scott says that Winthrop's sermon represented "a Christian model of commerce built on the radical precept of divine love. The entire text of the sermon is about business ethics, about the importance of the gospel changing the way we view how we actually live at the office."[41]

Scott continues:

> The Christian piety of Puritanism pervaded society to a large degree because Integrationists extended the development of their Christian mind to include its practical applications to the working occupations. A great tragedy of the current meta-physical void in the Christian worldview is the loss of this Christian understanding of work and vocation.[42]

Because of this void, instead of the church discipling our nations, the nations disciple the church. Because the church has lost the Puritan vision for education, she lacks the theological foundation for nation discipling. The process looks something like this: The church tries to speak relevantly to the culture and thus often adopts the language of the culture. Then she makes accommodation to the culture and ultimately is held captive by the culture.

For the church to disciple the nation, she must be rooted and grounded in truth and the circle of knowledge. The language of Scripture should be the language of discourse; theological language is to shape the mind and speech. The church, rather than accommodating culture, needs to call the nation to kingdom culture and the pursuit of truth, beauty, and goodness. The church is to be the force for emancipating the city and the nation to live in freedom in the marketplace and the public square.

Christian Overman says that this pursuit involves an unlikely word—*governance*, the idea that people serve the heavenly King as stewards exercising authority in His stead.

> Work, at its core, is an act of governance. Governance over wood, metal, cows, cotton, and carrots. Governance over sound waves, electrical currents, and wind. Governance over computer keyboards, fiber optics, and digital images. Governance over people. Governance over things. Governance over ideas.[43]

God is the God of the ordinary as well as the extraordinary. His hand is equally evident in a field of flowers and in a billion galaxies. For the Puritans, every act of life and work was sacred. This was a reflection of the Hebrew concept of דָבַ (*avodah*). This word, found 289 times in the Old Testament, is translated variously "work," "worship," and "service." There was no modern dichotomy in the Hebrew mind between pursuing one's vocation during the workweek and worshipping God on the appointed day. Work *was* worship. You expected to both find God in your workplace and to worship God in your work. This is the concept of vocation, a concept the Puritans lived out in their daily lives.

Leland Ryken of Wheaton College writes in his book *Worldly Saints*,

> The Puritans were par excellence the people who saw God in everyday events. They wrote diaries in which they traced God's grace in their daily lives. They confidently expected to find God in "the milk-house, the stable, the barn, and the like, where God [visits] the soul."[44]

Education as a means simply to acquire knowledge or technical skills in order to get a job, as so many see it today, is not an adequate vision for living a full, well-rounded life. John Dewey (1859–1952), regarded by many as the founder of America's modern education system, saw education as the way that students were to acquire technical skills so they could fit into a consumer society. A secularist, Dewey sought to remove from the public schools all references to God. The modern emphasis on STEM (science, technology, engineering, and mathematics) may prepare people for higher paying careers, but it does not prepare people for life.

Thus was the robust, practical Puritan vision of *technologia* reduced to knowing things and gaining skills to participate in the global consumer economy. While the premodern, Judeo-Christian world saw everything as connected to everything else, in the postmodern world everything means exactly nothing. It is past time to return to the Judeo-Christian vision—not of schooling, but of *education*.

Nations are either moving toward human flourishing and human freedom or toward growth in corruption and lawlessness leading to the rise of tyranny to restore a semblance of social order and peace. As we witness in totalitarian societies like China, North Korea, and Russia, non-conformists are taken to concentration camps and indoctrination camps until they sufficiently conform to group thought and behavior. We see this In the USA today, where people are forced to take courses that reorient their thinking regarding proper language for neo-pagan and postmodern sensibilities including how you must speak in proper gender identity and LGBT terms.

This will increasingly be the norm. This is the movement by which free citizens begin to revive the Puritan theology of education, in contrast to the state-sponsored atheistic assumptions. Then with this reform on the cultural level, attention can be placed on rebuilding on the institutional level, establishing educational policy and curriculum pedagogy in a variety of educational forms—home education, charter, parochial, and private educational models founded on the principles of *technologia*.

Let's begin the reform today!

In the next article, Dr. Elizabeth Youmans will remind us to think profoundly on the nature of the child. Children are born the Imago Dei and are filled with God-given potential. This profound understanding is essential to creating educational institutions that will educate the whole child and prepare him for God's purpose.

DARROW L. MILLER, who wrote Chapter One, is co-founder of the Disciple Nations Alliance and a featured author and teacher. For more than 25 years, Darrow has been a popular conference speaker on topics that include Christianity and culture, apologetics, worldview, poverty, and the dignity of women. From 1981 to 2007, Darrow worked with Food for the Hungry, serving from 1994 as vice president. Before joining FH, Darrow spent three years on staff at L'Abri Fellowship in Switzerland, where he was discipled by Francis Schaeffer.

He also served as a student pastor at Northern Arizona University and for two years as a pastor of Sherman Street Fellowship in urban Denver. In addition to earning his master's degree in adult education from Arizona State University, Darrow pursued graduate studies in philosophy, theology, Christian apologetics, biblical studies, and missions in the United States, Israel, and Switzerland.

Darrow has written numerous studies, articles, Bible studies and books, including *Discipling Nations: The Power of Truth to Transform Cultures*; *Nurturing the Nations: Reclaiming the Dignity of Women in Building Healthy Cultures*; *Servanthood: The Calling of Every Christian*; *LifeWork: A Biblical Theology for What You Do Every Day*; *Emancipating the World: A Christian Response to Radical Islam and Fundamentalist Atheism*; *Recovering Our Mission: Making the Invisible Kingdom Visible*; and *A Toxic New Religion: Understanding the Postmodern, Neo-Marxist Faith that Seeks to Destroy the Judeo-Christian Culture of the West.* Darrow is the General Editor of this compendium.

The Disciple Nations Alliance exists to serve the church, helping her rise to her full potential as God's principal agent in restoring, healing, and blessing broken nations. DNA emphasizes that Jesus is King, and His primary agenda is to advance the kingdom of God by discipling all nations. The key agent in this task is the local church, ministering wholistically and incarnationally and operating intentionally from a biblical worldview.

Disciple Nations Alliance, Secretariat Office, 1110 E. Missouri Ave., #393, Phoenix, Arizona 85014; Tel.: 602-386-4560; Fax: 602-386-4564; info@disciplenations.org; *disciplenations.org.*

TWO

The Christian View of Children

Elizabeth L. Youmans

> And they were bringing children to him that he might SG-2a
> touch them, and the disciples rebuked them. But when Jesus saw it, he was indignant and said to them, "Let the children come to me; do not hinder them, for to such belongs the kingdom of God. Truly, I say to you, whoever does not receive the kingdom of God like a child shall not enter it." And he took them in his arms and blessed them, laying his hands on them. (Mark 10:13–16)

The Plight of Children Today

A culture can be judged by the way it treats its children. A culture is really a reflection of the values and practices of the prevailing "religion" of a society. Today, most cultures have a pagan or secular view of children. Incredibly, children are despised in increasing numbers around the world, and never in the history of humankind have more babies been aborted, abandoned (both physically and psychologically), abused, violated, exploited, or exposed to famine, violence, disease, HIV-AIDS, and armed conflict than in this century. This rising generation is a "fatherless generation": unwanted, unloved, deserted, and unsupported physically, spiritually, and emotionally. Even when fathers are present, they spend on the average less than five minutes a day with their children.

According to recent demographics, 58 percent of the world's population is under the age of 25, and in the two-thirds world half the population is under the age of 15.[1] One in two children all over the world (one billion) lives in poverty. There are reportedly 640 million children without adequate shelter, 400 million with no access to safe water,[2] and 149 million who suffer from malnutrition. Millions of children are out of school because of poverty, discrimination, or lack of resources. There are over 100 million children who live, work, and sleep on the city streets.[3] On a daily basis, many go missing; are enlisted as soldiers; exploited in sex traffic; and, unbelievably, shot by the policemen hired to protect them. Their communities are extremely poor, and educational resources and economic opportunities simply do not exist for them.

Most children are out of sight and out of mind! Sadly, the Christian church ranks children as third-rate citizens in many cultures, while mothers are not taught how to nurture their young with Christian principles and ideals. We need the spirit of Elijah in this century. We need the hearts of fathers turned back to their children and those of the children to their fathers:

> Behold, I will send you Elijah the prophet before the great and terrible day of the Lord comes.
>
> And he shall turn and reconcile the hearts of the [estranged] fathers to the [ungodly] children, and the hearts of the [rebellious] children to [the piety of] their fathers [a reconciliation produced by repentance of the ungodly], lest I come and smite the land with a curse and a ban of utter destruction. (Malachi 4:5–6, AMPC)

Many philanthropic organizations, including international NGOs, and the Christian church reach out to millions of children each year and provide them shelter, food, clothing, and often the gospel. Few disciple children, however. Fewer still have the vision or capacity to *inspire* greatness in children or *teach* them how to reason with the transforming truth of God's Word for renewed minds and the cultivation of the Christian imagination for creative expression and godly problem solving.

Therefore, the cycle of ignorance and the poverty of biblical principles continue to leave their nations untransformed by the power of God and in bondage to the world's system.

Two Views of Children in the Church

In the U.S. church today, there are two views of children: the "high" view and the "low" view. In the words of Dr. Berryman, "We idealize children and yet we demonize them. We celebrate a 'year of the child' and exclude children from worship. We value them, yet spend relatively little time or money on their needs. We tout evangelism to add members, but we do not count children already present in the church to be worth 'evangelizing' or even the hospitality we give to strangers."[4]

In general, I have found that the body of Christ around the world holds children in low esteem. In many cultures, children are treated as third-class citizens. In 2003 I taught a group of fifty evangelical pastors for a week in one African nation. They shared with me that in their culture fathers never eat meals with their children or spend individual time with them.

Very few pastors and Christian leaders around the world even have the education of children on their radar screen. Most pastors are busy with church expansion and church planting. In the United States, children's ministries receive at best a meager five to seven percent of the church budget, and on Sunday mornings children are dismissed from the church service and relegated to classrooms to be entertained by untrained volunteers.

The church has never fully developed a "theology of childhood." God's priority for systematic Bible instruction and discipleship of children (Deuteronomy 4–6) is an unknown in most churches and Christian families around the world, while, alarmingly, most Christian children attend government schools that impart a secular worldview. Many churches have fashioned their services to "come down" into the popular culture to meet young people where they are. The standard of dress, music, and language is lowered so that youth can be engaged and entertained in church. This is not a biblical view of children!

Why Is This So?

From early antiquity and even since the birth of the Christian church, most adults have looked "down on" children and discounted their spirituality because they are "mere children." This low view is a result of many factors, not the least of which is that the church has rarely held an esteemed view of children.

Just as sad, in many cultures the church does not esteem women, either. Women—the bearers and nurturers of children—are viewed and treated as second-class citizens and oppressed in many cultures. A woman's divine role in the home is to set the tone for family life and childrearing. She is the "first and primary teacher" in a newborn's life. The family is one of God's ordained spheres of government and meant to reflect His love. God created families and intended the family unit to be the basic building block of nations! A nation can only be as "healthy" as its families! A nation that oppresses its women and holds children in low esteem is spiritually unhealthy and most likely economically unstable.

The Christian View of the Child

Jesus had a remarkable view of children, so much so that He esteemed them as the "greatest in the kingdom of heaven" (Matthew 18:1–5). He loved them and interacted with them by holding them in His arms, blessing them, and healing them. He left for us a model to emulate. There are few references, however, in the Gospels that relate to Christ and children, and the Scriptures never define "child" or "childhood." Those that are there are worthy of our study and reflection. The concept of "childhood" is relative to time and place. The construct is cultural and ever changing. Historically, theologians have consulted the Scriptures about children, but rarely have they observed or studied children.

The word *child*, defined:

> CHILD, (n.) (1) The progeny of parents. (2) One created in the image of God who is young in grace (1 John 2:12); unfixed in principles (Galatians 4:3; Ephesians 4:14; Proverbs 1:4); and weak in knowledge, judgment, and experience (Jeremiah 1:6). (Webster's 1828 Dictionary)

> Every child is a promise—
> With a name, a passion, a story,
> And a place in HIS Story!

Every child is unique! There are no "ordinary" children (see Hebrews 11:23, NIV).

> Don't let anyone look down on you because you are young, but set an example for the believers in speech, in conduct, in love, in faith and in purity. (1 Timothy 4:12)

Biblical Principles that Undergird the Christian View of Children

1. Children are a gift from God to parents, who are to nurture them and train them up in the admonition of the Lord.

> Children are a heritage from the LORD. (Psalm 127:3)

> Fathers, do not exasperate your children; instead, bring them up in the training and instruction of the Lord. (Ephesians 6:4)

2. Each child is made in God's image and destined for immortality. Each has great potential, creativity, greatness, the capacity to think, reason, love, and learn.

> Then God said, "Let us make man in our image, after our likeness. And let them have dominion over the fish of the sea and over the birds of the heavens and over the livestock and over all the earth and over every creeping thing that creeps on the earth."

> So God created man in his own image,
> in the image of God he created him;
> male and female he created them. (Genesis 1:26–27)

> I praise you, for I am fearfully and wonderfully made.
> Wonderful are your works;
> my soul knows it very well.
> My frame was not hidden from you,
> when I was being made in secret,
> intricately woven in the depths of the earth. (Psalm 139:14–15)

3. Each child is ennobled with dignity and worth! In the eye of God, all children are equal. Each child is imputed with independent value apart from his station in life or his abilities.

> What is man that you are mindful of him,
> and the son of man that you care for him?
> Yet You have made him a little lower than the heavenly beings
> and crowned him with glory and honor.
> You have given him dominion over the works of your hands;

> You have put all things under his feet. (Psalm 8:4–6)

> But even the hairs of your head are all numbered. Fear not, therefore; you are of more value than many sparrows. (Matthew 10:30–31)

4. Each child is fashioned by God for an appointed time and place in His story.

> The God who created the world and everything in it, since He is Lord of heaven and earth, does not dwell in temples made with hands; nor is He served by human hands, as though He needed anything, because it is He who gives to all [people] life and breath and all things. And He made from one man every nation of mankind to live on the face of the earth, *having determined their appointed times and the boundaries of their lands and territories. This was so that they would seek God*, if perhaps they might grasp for Him and find Him, though He is not far from each one of us. For in Him we live and move and exist [that is, in Him we actually have our being], as even some of your own poets have said, 'For we also are His children.' So then, being God's children, we should not think that the Divine Nature (deity) is like gold or silver or stone, an image formed by the art and imagination or skill of man. (Acts 17:24–29, AMP, emphasis added)

5. God has a plan for each child's life.

> Before I formed you [Jeremiah] in the womb, I knew you, and before you were born I consecrated you. (Jeremiah 1:5)

> Your eyes saw my unformed substance;
> in your book were all written, every one of them,
> the days that were formed for me,
> when as yet there was none of them.
> How precious to me are your thoughts, O God!
> How vast is the sum of them! (Psalm 139:16–17)

> For behold, you shall conceive and bear a son. No razor shall come upon his head, for the child [Samson] shall be a Nazirite to God from the womb; and he shall begin to save Israel from the hand of the Philistines. (Judges 13:5)

> But . . . [God] who had set me [Paul] apart before I was born, and who called me by his grace, was pleased to reveal his Son to me, in order that I might preach him among the Gentiles. (Galatians 1:15–16)

6. Each child has inalienable rights and, therefore, responsibilities to steward his internal property, conscience, and a providential calling.

> But the angel said to him, "Do not be afraid, Zechariah, for your prayer has been heard, and your wife Elizabeth will bear you a son, and you shall call his name John. And you will have joy and gladness, and many will rejoice at his birth, for he will be great before the Lord. And he must not drink wine or strong drink, and he will be filled with the Holy Spirit, even from his mother's womb. And he will turn many of the children of Israel to the Lord their God, and he will go before him in the spirit and power of Elijah, to turn the hearts of the fathers to the children, and the disobedient to the wisdom of the just, to make ready for the Lord a people prepared." (Luke 1:13–17)

7. The primary educators in a child's life are his parents, who should seek the Lord to know how to guide and train him.

> For I have chosen him [Abraham], that he may command his children and his household after him to keep the way of the Lord by doing righteousness and justice, so that the Lord may bring to Abraham what he has promised him. (Genesis 18:19)

> You shall teach them diligently to your children, and shall talk of them when you sit in your house, and when you walk by the way, and when you lie down, and when you rise up. (Deuteronomy 6:7)

> Train up a child in the way he should go;
> even when he is old he will not depart from it. (Proverbs 22:6)

> I have no greater joy than to hear that my children are walking in the truth. (3 John 4)

8. Jesus eagerly received children unto Himself and called them "the greatest in the kingdom of God."

> At that time the disciples came to Jesus, saying, "Who is the greatest in the kingdom of heaven?" And calling to him a child, he put him in the midst of them and said, "Truly, I say to you, unless you turn and become like children, you will never enter the kingdom of heaven. *Whoever humbles himself like this child is the greatest in the kingdom of heaven.*
> "Whoever receives one such child in my name receives me." (Matthew 18:1–5, emphasis added)

> And they were bringing children to him that he might touch them, and the disciples rebuked them. But when Jesus saw it, he was indignant and said to them, "Let the children come to me; do not hinder them, for to such belongs the kingdom of God. Truly, I say to you, whoever does not receive the kingdom of God like a child shall not enter it." And he took them in his arms and blessed them, laying his hands on them." (Mark 10:13–16)

I Am God's Workmanship

Rosalie J. Slater

God made me special,
Like no one else you see.
He made me a witness
To His diversity.
God made me for His purpose,
He fashioned me to be
An image for His glory,
Almighty Father He.[5]

Two Educational Views of Children

	Traditional View	Transformational View
Child Is Seen:	Blank; empty Few are gifted and talented	Full; made in God's image Each is talented and creative
Goal:	Behavior modification	Heart transformed Attain the full stature of Christ
Classroom Governance:	Dependent upon others Leveled Consumers of facts	Independent learners Mastery of subjects Independently productive
Methods:	Appeal to the external Entertain and control	Appeal to the internal Inspire and consecrate
Curriculum:	Language dumbed down Piecemeal, fragmented Driven by rote memorization of facts Secular worldview	Elevated language; biblical imagery Whole Taught by principles Biblical, Christian worldview
Result:	Socialization of the child	Reaching his full potential and expression of his value in Christ

Principles of Nurturing Children Christianly

A definition for children is *those young in grace, unfixed in principles, and weak in knowledge, judgment, and experience.* Children are weak and frail physically when compared with adults. They are dependent upon the care of those to whom they are entrusted. They cannot choose the company under whose influence they come. They need the unconditional love of their parents and teachers to feed, nurture, tend, and guide them every day. However, a child was placed by Christ as a model for adults to imitate, because a child's spirit is generally unencumbered (unless the child has been abused and/or abandoned) and easily receives eternal truths.

1. A child is a gift from God and entrusted to parents. Each child bears the imprint of God's individuality and is ennobled with great potential. It is the responsibility of parents and teachers to call forth and affirm this potential.

> Behold, children are a heritage from the Lord,
>   the fruit of the womb a reward.
> Like arrows in the hand of a warrior
>   are the children of one's youth.
> Blessed is the man
>   who fills his quiver with them!
> He shall not be put to shame
>   when he speaks with his enemies in the gate. (Psalm 127:3–5)

2. A child needs a "mother" who loves and nourishes his soul with acceptance and the pure milk of the Word of God:

> Like newborn babies, long for the pure spiritual milk, that by it you may grow up into salvation. (1 Peter 2:2)

> If you put these things before the brothers, you will be a good servant of Christ Jesus, being trained in the words of the faith and of the good doctrine that you have followed. (1 Timothy 4:6)

> Oh, taste and see that the Lord is good!
>   Blessed is the man who takes refuge in him! (Psalm 34:8)

3. A child needs a "father" who guides and guards him and blesses him daily. Blessing is a biblical ethic. God blessed Adam and Eve. God blessed Abraham. He in turn blessed his children, and they in turn blessed their children. Blessing children is rooted in the nature of our heavenly Father. Blessing

heals and sustains life and relationships! The ethic of blessing is personal. Being unblessed is to live restlessly and inadequately with an inner poverty!

> I [God] will bless those who bless you [Abraham], and him who dishonors you I will curse, and in you all the families of the earth shall be blessed. (Genesis 12:3)

> Christ redeemed us from the curse of the law by becoming a curse for us—for it is written, "Cursed is everyone who is hanged on a tree"—so that in Christ Jesus the blessing of Abraham might come to the Gentiles, so that we might receive the promised Spirit through faith. (Galatians 3:13–14)

> Finally, all of you, have unity of mind, sympathy, brotherly love, a tender heart, and a humble mind. Do not repay evil for evil or reviling for reviling, but on the contrary, bless, for to this you were called, that you may obtain a blessing. (1 Peter 3:8–9)

4. Every child needs unconditional love, which God has provided through His Son (John 3:16).

5. Every child is a sinner and needs a Savior. Introduce children to the Creator and His creation, and teach them the doctrines of Christianity. This is the first step to "becoming" what God intends us to be.
   - Becoming is a lifelong process. The soul should be restored in accordance with new life in Christ.
   - Teach and practice Christianity as an incarnational religion—truth embodied in a physical world that contains elements of design (form, shape, line, color), as well as truth embodied in real people to whom God gave the ability to respond to beauty by His grace.
   - Teach the providence of God in history. God has a special plan and purpose for every child.

6. Every child needs a vision for what he can become, and someone to cultivate his individuality, call it forth, and believe in it with him! Every child is unique with a divine calling and a unique learning style that must be embraced, understood, and instructed.

> Then Manoah entreated the LORD and said, "O LORD, please let the man of God whom you sent come to us and *teach us what we are to do with the child who will be born*." And God listened to the voice of Manoah, and the angel of God came again to the woman as she sat in the field. But Manoah her husband was not with her. So the woman ran quickly and told her husband, "Behold, the man who came to me the other day has appeared to me." And Manoah arose and went after his wife and came to the man and said to him, "Are you the man who spoke to this woman?" And he said, "I am." And Manoah said, "Now when your words come true, what is to be the child's manner of life, and what is his mission?" And the angel of the Lord said to Manoah, "Of all that I said to the woman let her be careful." (Judges 13:8–13, emphasis added)

7. The Christian approach to nurturing children must embrace a wholistic (see discussion in Chapter Five, page 97, regarding the unique spelling of this word [generally "holistic"] used throughout this book) view, not a dualistic one:
   - Every child should be seen through the eyes of God, the Creator.
   - Teach the whole child (the Hebrew view: heart, mind, spirit, and body).
   - Teach the child how to integrate thinking and acting—how to be whole! What is his potential in Christ? Call him to that potential.
   - Teach subjects holistically in the unity of truth.

God builds from the inside out! The internal always gives rise to the external. Life flows out from the heart. The heart is our "command center" and governs our will and all our choices and decisions.

> The LORD said to Samuel, "Do not look on his appearance or the height of his stature, because I have rejected him. For the LORD sees not as man sees: man looks on the outward appearance, but the LORD looks at the heart." (1 Samuel 16:7)

> Keep your heart with all vigilance,
> for from it flow the springs of life. (Proverbs 4:23)

> The good person out of the good treasure of his heart produces good, and the evil person out of his evil treasure produces evil, for out of the abundance of the heart his mouth speaks. (Luke 6:45)

8. Every child has a will with which to govern his thinking, choices, decisions, conduct, and property.
   - Children must be instructed with God's law and moral principles.
   - A child has choices that can be exercised by his will. He can at least to a degree decide what his existence will be. He is not locked into a life of poverty and oppression. The domain of the will is not a choice between *things*, but a *choice between ideas*! Ideas have consequences.
   - Incarnational principle: Jesus's life, mind, and character dwell within the believer. A child can be taught how to choose life! This opposes the behavioral modification theory: "Environment shapes the individual." Character must be taught as causative, not as the byproduct of one's circumstances and environment. Humans are not victims of their environment!
   - Parents and teachers must teach and model virtuous ideals and biblical principles.
   - Give the will an object outside itself, and it will leap into action! The key: Where is the child's mind focused?

> As he thinks within himself, so is he. (Proverbs 23:7, NASB)

9. Every child has "internal property" that must be carefully stewarded.
   - heart: determines behavior
   - intellect and gift of reason
   - conscience: tells him right from wrong
   - will: seat of decision making
   - character: fruit of her choices
   - imagination/ideas: intellectual property
   - temperament/emotions
   - gifts and abilities
   - worldview
   - sexual identity

10. A child's "receptive mind," or the seat of his imagination and intuition, must be lovingly nurtured with truth and beauty! God created human beings with an imagination, and He reveals His attributes of beauty and truth throughout His creation! *Learning begins in the imagination, where thought and experience come together.* A child's aesthetic tastes and sensibilities need to be cultivated through universal stories and the fine and performing arts that portray Christian ideals and virtues. If parents and teachers don't actively cultivate a Christian imagination, the devil will cultivate the child's imagination for his purposes! Man is a doer of deeds and a dreamer of dreams.

11. God endowed humanity with the gift of language with which to praise and worship Him and communicate ideas and blessings to others. The "law of kindness" should be the standard for the tongue that communicates with children.

> Death and life are in the power of the tongue,
> and those who love it will eat its fruits. (Proverbs 18:21)

> She opens her mouth with wisdom,
> and the teaching of kindness is on her tongue. . . .
> Her children rise up and call her blessed. (Proverbs 31:26, 28)

12. Children need biblical truths and biblical vocabulary as the foundation upon which to imagine, think, and reason Christianly in every area of life.

> Do not be conformed to this world, but be transformed by the renewal of your mind, that by testing you may discern what is the will of God, what is good and acceptable and perfect. (Romans 12:2)

13. Adults must "see" and "hear" what children are communicating! Nonverbal communication is found in our human spirituality. Look and listen to children with your spiritual eyes and ears, as well as your physical eyes and ears.

Nurturing and Guarding the Child's Inner Life[6]

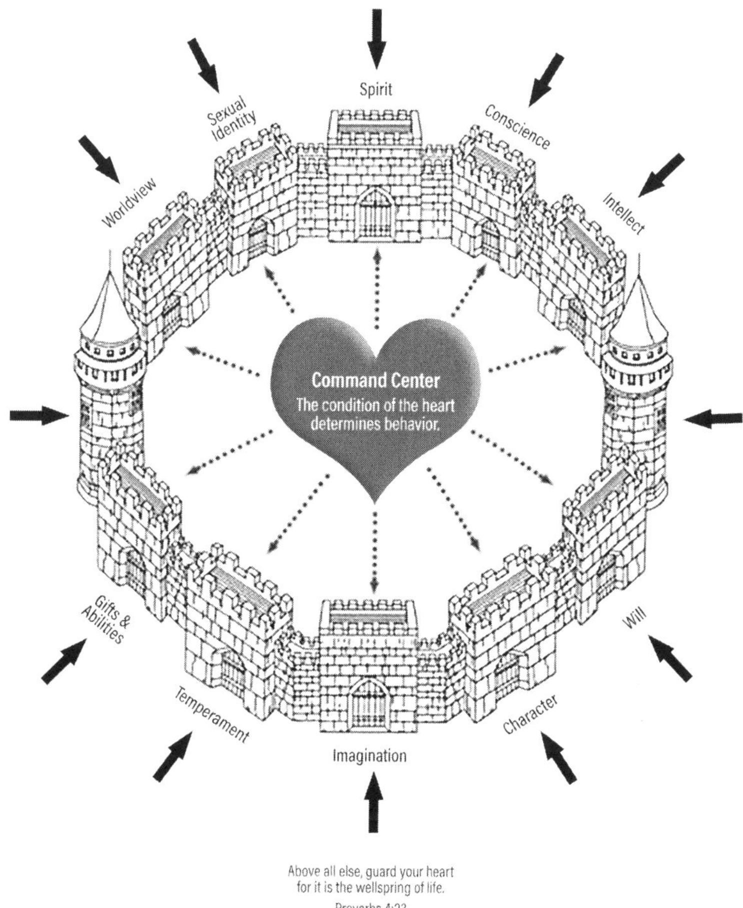

Above all else, guard your heart
for it is the wellspring of life.
Proverbs 4:23

The next article looks at the essential role of the Bible in early American education. The biblical worldview was the founding framework for establishing a unique nation of a free and self-governing people. The Bible itself was the integration point of early education in what became the United States; it produced a biblically literate population and several generations of political, educational, and business leaders.

Elizabeth L. Youmans, who wrote chapters 2 and 3, has served North American Christian education as a classroom teacher, school administrator, trainer of teachers, graduate school professor, curriculum writer, and editor of The Noah Plan®, a K-12 published day school and homeschool curriculum. Dr. Youmans founded and now governs a Christian educational institute called Chrysalis International in Orlando, Florida. With thirty years of pioneering experience in Word-centered education at the local and national levels, she now imparts the vision for educational transformation internationally by laying teaching and learning solidly on the foundation of Christ and His Word. Challenged in 2002 by an international NGO to create a principle-based curriculum for at-risk children around the world, she designed and now writes and edits the curriculum for AMO® Program, an enriched children's curriculum and worldview training courses for home and church that is translated into Spanish, Portuguese, and French for use throughout the world.

Chrysalis International, Inc. is a nonprofit educational institute that disciples Christian leaders around the world who are called to break the cycle of ignorance and the poverty of ideas in the church by teaching the knowledge and application of biblical principles for education and self-government to transform the culture for Christ.

Chrysalis also provides Christian Education Vision conferences and teacher training programs based on a nation-building model that lays Christ and His Word as the foundation for renewing the mind; building a biblical, Christian worldview; and inspiring fresh vision to transform education. In addition, Chrysalis serves leaders and school founders through individual consultations and discipleship.

AMO Program: *training.amoprogram.com*

Chrysalis International, Inc. 263 Wexford Court, Altamonte Springs, FL 32714; Tel: 321-422-0739; info@chrysalisinternational.org; *training.amoprogram.com/about/mission*

Bibliography

Adams, Carole. 1991. "The Christian Idea of the Child." *F.A.C.E. Journal* (2). San Francisco, CA: Foundation for American Christian Education.

Articles and statistics about children gathered from world and U.S. agencies: *caster.ssw.upenn.edu/~restes/praxis/kidlinks.html.*

Barclay, William. 1959. *Educational Ideals in the Ancient World.* Grand Rapids: Baker Book House.

Bunge, Marcia J., ed. 2001. *The Child in Christian Thought.* Grand Rapids: Eerdmans.

Forbes, Cheryl. 1986. *Imagination: Embracing a Theology of Wonder.* Portland, OR: Multnomah Press.

Glaspey, Terry. 1995. *Children of a Greater God.* Eugene, OR: Harvest House Publishers.

Miller, Darrow. 2008. *Nurturing the Nations: Reclaiming the Dignity of Women in Building Healthy Cultures.* Colorado Springs, CO: Paternoster Publishing.

Stormer, John. 1984. *Growing Up God's Way.* Florissant, MO: Liberty Bell Press.

Tripp, Tedd. 1995. *Shepherding a Child's Heart.* Wapwallopen, PA: Shepherd Press.

Weber, Hans-Ruedi. 1979. *Jesus and the Children.* Atlanta, GA: John Knox Press.

Wilson, Marin. 1989. *Our Father Abraham: Jewish Roots of the Christian Faith.* Grand Rapids: Eerdmans.

Youmans, Elizabeth L., Jill C. Thrift, and Scott D. Allen. 2013. *As the Family Goes, So Goes the Nation.* Orlando, FL: Chrysalis International, Inc. and Phoenix, AZ: Disciple Nations Alliance.

THREE

The Remarkable Role of the Bible in Early American Education

Elizabeth L. Youmans

Before the North American colonies became "these United States," parents understood their divine mandate to early instruct their children. As descendants of the European Reformers, who highly valued a "virtuous education of youths,"[1] the colonials believed the education of their children was a generational duty to form the future and its leadership upon the foundation of Christ and His Word. Founding Father Samuel Adams wrote, 

> Let divines and philosophers, statesmen and patriots, unite their endeavors to renovate the age, by . . . educating their little boys and girls . . . and instructing them in the art of self-government, without which they never can act a wise part in the government of societies, great or small; in short of leading them in the study and practice of the exalted virtues of the Christian system.[2]

Many families who sailed west were Calvinists, whom historians later referred to as "people of the Book." Their pastors had taught them how to reason justly with the revelation of God's Word in the civil realm. Geneva was Calvin's great experiment in Christian civil government. He also focused on providing a quality Christian education for Geneva's citizens, noting that an educated laity is essential for a strong church. *Throughout the history of Christianity, wherever the gospel has taken root, Christian education follows, and literacy rises significantly with the reading of God's Word.*

In 1620, out of concern for their children's future, the Pilgrims departed Holland for America with the Geneva Bible under their arms. The Geneva Bible contains the marginal notes of the sixteenth-century Reformers who sought refuge in Geneva at that time. Those notes included commentary about civil government that so frightened King James I that he banned the Geneva Bible in England and commissioned his own translation, declaring, "There will be no marginal notes in my Bible!"

During the 150 years when America was a collection of English colonies, children were home-schooled. Parents took seriously their role to not only teach their children how to read, write, and cipher but to cultivate virtuous character and Christian conscience for future citizenry. The Bible was their primer, and children were catechized. John Locke characterized the reading curriculum of the American colonies as "the ordinary road of Hornbook, Primer, Psalter, Testament, and Bible."[3] After home education, many colonial boys attended grammar school and were taught Latin, the language of scholarship, by their local pastors.

Wealthy families often sent their sons to England to receive a more formal, classical education in their well-established academies and universities. However, as colleges were founded in North America, others availed themselves of this new option. These choices would prove influential in the building of a new nation. It is providential that *none of the colonials schooled in England helped draft the Declaration of Independence, the U.S. Constitution, and the Bill of Rights. These great documents of liberty were the harvest of colonial education.* John Adams, Thomas Jefferson, and Benjamin Franklin all had a part in drafting the Declaration of Independence (1776). James Madison, who was educated at the College of New Jersey in Reformation theology, was the architect of the U.S. Constitution (1787) and the Bill of Rights (1789).

George Washington, president of the Constitutional Convention, was home-schooled on his family's farm by his father, who died when George was only 11 years old. His stepbrother taught him for several years. His only formal education was a course of instruction in surveying. In 1775, Washington's first official act as Commander-in-Chief of the Continental Army was to commission a chaplain corps to attend to the spiritual needs of his soldiers. As "Father of His Country," he is often called the "Moses of America." In his lifetime, Washington wrote over forty volumes of personal correspondence, in addition to a vast number of volumes of state papers as president of the new nation. His letters are highly inspiring, and his understanding of Christian self- and civil government was biblical. His "Farewell Address" (1796) is a lesson on the importance of religion and morality in politics and of the need of the 13 new states to maintain unity for the future health of the United States. It is considered one of the more important historical documents of the new republic.

Noah Webster, the colonial attorney and schoolmaster who wrote the 1828 *American Dictionary of the English Language*, is called the "Father of American Education." His scholarship set the standard in the new nation for many generations. Webster was also educated in the colonies. His father so prized education that he mortgaged the family farm to send Noah to Yale College! While reading for the law, Noah Webster taught school and tutored youth for entrance into college. Later, he waged a long battle to see the U.S. Constitution ratified in all the new states. As he traveled, he stopped at Mount Vernon to visit George Washington. While there, he chastised Washington for hiring tutors from England to teach Martha's grandchildren!

At the age of fifty, Webster tackled the writing of the first American dictionary, a task that required the mastery of 26 languages. He wanted to provide the new nation with her own dictionary. He understood that words are the building blocks of ideas. The colonies had fought eight years to win independence from England in order to be self-governing under God.

Webster believed it was important to provide definitions that communicated the worldview of the U.S. Constitution and its underlying Christian principles of liberty and civil governance. In addition to researching the root meanings of words, he also researched words in the Hebrew and Greek lexicons and defined them according to how they were used in Scripture. Some of his entries have as many as twenty definitions based on the fine nuances of meaning found in the Bible! (As an example, look up the word "serve."[4]) *Webster's 1828 is the only dictionary in the world that includes biblical meanings of words.*

Webster founded Amherst College and fought for universal education in the nation. More than any other of his day, he understood the power of words and the consequences of ideas! Several relevant Webster quotes include:

> In my view, the Christian religion is the most important and one of the first things in which all children under a free government ought to be instructed. . . . No truth is more evident to my mind than that the Christian religion must be the basis of any government intended to secure the rights and privileges of a free people.[5]

Education is useless without the Bible.

> When you become entitled to exercise the right of voting for public officers, let it be impressed on your mind that God commands you to choose for rulers, 'just men who will rule in the fear of God.' The preservation of [our] government depends on the faithful discharge of this Duty; if the citizens neglect their Duty and place unprincipled men in office, the government will soon be corrupted; laws will be made, not for the public good so much as for selfish or local purposes; corrupt or incompetent men will be appointed to execute the Laws; the public revenues will be squandered on unworthy men; and the rights of the citizen will be violated or disregarded. If [our] government fails to secure public prosperity and happiness, it must be because the citizens neglect the Divine Commands, and elect bad men to make and administer the Laws.[6]

Besides his American dictionary, which took him over twenty years to complete, Webster authored the *Blue-Backed Spelling Book*, grammar and history texts, catechisms, and in his later years an American translation of the Bible (1833). As an educator, Webster was interested in the connection of the Bible to all fields of study and desired an accurate translation in English. Although it is still in print today, his translation did not receive wide acceptance due to the continued popularity of the King James Version. For Webster, his translation was the work that meant the most to him, and in 1834 he published a companion piece for parents to use with their children, titled *Value of the Bible and Excellence of the Christian Religion: For the Use of Families and Schools*. At the conclusion he wrote:

> The Christian religion exalts the intellect and perfects the human character. The sublime views of God and of his works,

> which the scriptures exhibit, have a wonderful effect in strengthening the intellect and expanding its powers. . . . Equally effectual are the scriptures in refining our ideas, by representations of purity and holiness of God. The more we know of God, the more just will be our concepts of what is ennobling in our own conduct; and every step we take in imitation of his perfections is an advance in elevation of character. This purity of mind, and this elevation and expansion of intellect are the beginnings of that ever-increasing holiness, and that boundless enlargement of knowledge, which are to complete the character and the felicity of the children of God, in another world.

The record of colonial education in America, with the Bible as its primer, validates an important principle: The greatest foundations for building Christian culture are the knowledge of God's Word and the ability to think and reason with its truths.

> All Scripture is breathed out by God and profitable for teaching, for reproof, for correction, and for training in righteousness, that the man of God may be complete, equipped for every good work. (2 Timothy 3:16–17).

Christ-Centered Education Produces Leaders

> Let every student be plainly instructed, and earnestly pressed to consider well the maine end of his life and studies is to know God and Jesus Christ, which is eternal life (Joh.17.3) and therefore to lay Christ in the bottome, as the only foundation of all sound knowledge and learning.[7] (a portion of Harvard College's Mission Statement, 1643)

The first call for education in the Bible is found in Genesis 18:18–19: "Abraham shall surely become a great and mighty nation, and all the nations of the earth will be blessed in him. For I have chosen him, that he may command his children and his household after him to keep the way of the Lord by doing righteousness and justice, so that the Lord may bring to Abraham what he has promised him." This is the heart of our heavenly Father addressing the heart of an earthly father to train up his children in the ways of God, so that his family and future nation will be blessed and will, in turn, bless all nations. God gave the responsibility for educating children in the nurture of the Lord to parents.

The cornerstone of early American education was the belief that "children are a heritage from the LORD" (Psalm 127:3a). America's colonial period reflects the fruit of parents who took seriously their role to provide their progeny a godly education, as well as a Christian model for righteous living. Like the practice of the ancient Jews, education and discipleship began in the home at mother's knee and often ended in the cornfield or the silversmith's shop apprenticing with the father. Most colonial families had a copy of the Bible and attended church regularly. Dr. Lawrence A. Cremin, a distinguished scholar in the field of education, wrote that during America's colonial period the Bible was "the single most important cultural influence in the lives of Anglo-Americans."[8] Parents taught the rising generation to think and reason with biblical principles, which prepared them to establish the world's first Christian constitutional republic. Another word for "constitution" is *covenant*. The propagation of God's covenant promises to Abraham has been dependent upon parents teaching the next generation His commandments and ways.

America's First 150 Years Provide a Strong Model of Education

Eighteenth-century clergymen were also instrumental in preparing the colonists in their struggle for independence from Mother England, a monarchy whose king violated their individual rights as English citizens. It was the clergy's vigorous preaching and active participation in the war itself that gave the religious sanction and inspiration for the writing of the Declaration of Independence, the United States Constitution, and the Bill of Rights. Those first 150 years produced a model of education worth replicating in the family and the church today.

As sovereign ruler of the universe and the author of human history, God governs in the affairs of men and nations. History is "His story." A Christian history timeline is a helpful tool to trace His providential hand in His story. It begins with creation and proceeds to the founding of the United States of America; her flowering as the first Christian constitutional republic; and, sadly, the erosion of her educational underpinnings and Christian character. Tracing God's hand highlights how He has used both key individuals and nations to move the gospel and its effect of internal and external liberty from Jerusalem to the remotest parts of the earth.

God has always placed a great emphasis on His people remembering His mighty acts and teaching the knowledge of them to the next generation (Psalm

78:1–7). Sadly, few Americans are aware that during the twentieth and twenty-first centuries, revisionist historians and secular educators have robbed them of knowing their Christian legacy by *intentionally* removing from textbooks all remembrance of God and His miraculous providence in the founding and constitutional eras. This has been a deliberate act to deprive Americans of their individual liberty. The American church, today, is in need of a "great awakening" from her ignorance and lethargy in order to recognize and own God's mandate for godly education and Christian discipleship. Too often, this mandate is met in the local church with an "educational" program for children designed to babysit and entertain them. Children hunger and thirst for righteousness and yearn for instruction that transcends the mediocrity and depravity of the popular culture to inspire their imaginations to nobleness of thought and deed.

This is precisely the testimony of Samuel, the child dedicated by his mother to education under the nurture of Israel's high priest and educator, Eli. Samuel knew firsthand the tragedy of the omission of godly education and the lack of role models in a nation. He had witnessed its effect in the moral degradation of his people. His solution, which birthed a great awakening in Israel, was to establish schools of the prophets to restore to his whole nation the study of God's Word and the knowledge of God in all subjects—in literature, history, natural science, and the arts. In only twenty years, Samuel's restoration of biblical education turned his nation back to God and established her character and identity as God's chosen people—a nation called to be a light unto the world!

Another biblical example of the role of godly education in deliverance from sin, oppression, and ignorance of God's Word is the reconstruction project of the civil governor Nehemiah and the high priest Ezra. After seventy years of exile in Babylon, the "Hollywood of the ancient empires," God sent them back to the desolate capital city. Nehemiah and the returning exiles, with the help of the local Jewish remnant, rebuilt the walls of Jerusalem in just 52 days! He then gathered all the families into the marketplace to listen to Ezra, the premier Jewish educator, read and teach the meaning of God's Law (Nehemiah 8:1–3). Those who had been left behind in Jerusalem after the Babylonian destruction had lost contact with God's Word. As Ezra opened the scroll and began to read, the people soon wept profusely, as God's living Word pierced their hearts. They cried out to God for forgiveness and repented. Nehemiah called for a festival, and the people joyously celebrated, "because they had understood the words that were declared to them" (Nehemiah 8:12). Ezra then taught them their glorious, providential history (Nehemiah 9). Their ignorance of God's miracles and guidance throughout the history of their nation had robbed them of their knowledge as a divinely chosen people. Once their understanding was illumined, they renewed God's covenant in writing. The reconstruction work was not complete until Jerusalem's families were rebuilt spiritually and her cultural institutions rested solidly on God's Law! God was consecrating His people, so that He could send His only Son to earth to atone for the sins of the world and fulfill His eternal plan for humankind.

All the great Protestant Reformers of the sixteenth century—Luther, Calvin, Knox, Zwingli, Sturm, Farel, Beza, and Melanchthon—were aggressive education champions committed to Bible-centered Christian instruction and discipleship. They understood that long-term church reform requires educational reform at all levels. Given their limited resources, their achievements were remarkable. Martin Luther, the young German monk who ignited the Reformation in 1517, laid the foundation for renovating the church's educational system. He was a strong advocate of Christian schools and Bible-centered learning. Luther promoted Christian education, not to gain church attendance or material wealth, but for the purpose of *preserving the integrity of the gospel of Christ.* He warned us in the sixteenth century,

> Above all, in schools of all kinds the chief and most common lesson should be in the Scriptures. . . . I am afraid that the universities will prove to be the great gates of hell unless they diligently labor in explaining the Holy Scriptures, engraving them in the hearts of youth. I advise no one to place his child where the Scriptures do not reign paramount. Every institution in which men are not increasingly occupied with the Word of God must become corrupt.[9]

John Calvin and John Knox were the foremost leaders of the second generation of evangelical Protestant Reformers. Their influence, particularly Calvin's, exceeded that of Luther. Both visionaries wrote educational plans—Calvin's was a citywide system for Geneva, and Knox's was a national system for his beloved Scotland.

Early American education bears the undeniable imprint of the Bible-centric educational philosophy of Calvin and Knox. Dr. Benjamin Rush—physician, co-founder of five colleges, signer of the Declaration of Independence, and founder of the Bible Society—was the first American founding father to propose free public schools. He thought children should actually read the Bible for themselves, not just have it read to them. He petitioned society that the Bible should be the primary textbook taught in public schools in his publication titled *A Defense of the Use of the Bible as a School Book* (1791):[10]

> Before I state my arguments in favor of teaching children to read by means of the Bible, I shall assume the following propositions: First, that Christianity is the only true and perfect religion, and that in proportion as mankind adopts its principles and obeys its precepts, they will be wise and happy; Second, that a better knowledge of this religion is to be acquired by reading the Bible than in any other way; Finally, that the Bible contains more knowledge necessary to man in his present state than any other book in the world. . . . I believe no man was ever early instructed in the truths of the Bible without having been made wiser or better by the early operation of these impressions upon his mind.

Today, many young Christians sit passively in front of computers filling in endless worksheets or drawing lines to the matching answers from curricula written by secular humanists. They have not plumbed the riches of the classics with a master teacher nor been taught the skills of composition and rhetoric. *It is writing that produces thinkers!* With a bankrupt vocabulary and no understanding of God's hand in the history of Western civilization, communication for the twenty-first-century student has been reduced to tweets, emojis, and selfies!

Webster's 1828 Dictionary, which contains biblical meanings of words, defines "education" as follows:

> EDUCATION (n.) [Latin: *educatio*, to lead out of.] The bringing up, as of a child, instruction; formation of manners. Education comprehends all that series of instruction and discipline which is intended to enlighten the understanding, correct the temper, and form the manners and habits of youth, and fit them for usefulness in their future stations. To give children a good education in manners, arts and science, is important; to give them a religious education is indispensable; and an immense responsibility rests on parents and guardians who neglect these duties.

Second Timothy 3:16–17 inspired this definition, which includes not only instruction but discipline. It contains four active verbs indicating that education is not meant to be the passive institution it has become in the last 100 years. With the onset of the information era, education has been reduced to memorizing facts (not truths) in order to pass the next test. This process bypasses the spirit of the mind, and information is soon forgotten. Students are left with a recognition mentality of subject content, not a mastery of the subject's principles, as in the colonial era. English apologist Dorothy Sayers wrote in her essay "The Lost Tools of Learning" that, "although we often succeed in teaching our pupils 'subjects,' we fail lamentably on the whole in teaching them how to think: They learn everything, except the art of learning."[11]

Education as God intended is teaching and learning. Teaching and learning, first and foremost, constitute a relationship. It is the heart-to-heart and mind-to-mind relationship between the teacher and the student that fosters both internal and eternal consequences. Children need teachers, not computers; masters of disciplines, not self-directed workbooks. The goal of Christian education is not the impartation of facts but changed lives! When the imagination is inspired by truth and beauty and the mind is actively engaged in thinking and reasoning that conforms to the Word of God, the Holy Spirit enlightens the student's understanding, and he joyfully learns for himself. "But it is a spirit in man, and the breath of the Almighty gives them understanding" (Job 32:8, NASB1995).

Dr. Rush made a bold claim in his essay that "teaching the Bible in schools would in the course of two generations, eradicate infidelity among us and render civil government scarcely necessary in our country."[12] My study of this essay years ago is what prompted me to design an enrichment program to restore to youth the lost virtues of beauty, truth, and moral goodness. This program nurtures children by reading aloud the great children's classics, by giving them a taste of Christian history, by cultivating Christian imagination through the arts, and by providing them a Bible to read for themselves. Every lesson is built on a biblical principle, and the children are guided to reason with and rightly apply truth to their own lives.[13] Hearts and minds are inspired, and the joy of learning is once again ignited. Christian imagination is cultivated to dream God-sized dreams and to wonder at His glorious creation and His overruling hand in their lives and nations. In the words of twentieth-century Christian educator Dr. Mark Fakkema,

> To educate the children of today is to construct the foundation of the nation tomorrow. Faithless teaching makes for un-

> faithful citizens. . . . We are in need of a nationwide education that honors God and teaches study content in the light of God's Word.[14]

The decay of America's culture cries out for the church to repent of her complacency and impart God's mandate for *generational duty*—the obligation of this generation as guardians and stewards of the nation to form the future leadership, and indeed the future, through Christ-centered education. 

The American Revolution Was Fueled by Preaching

From the mid-1600s to the mid-1800s, public schools as we know them today were virtually nonexistent. Parents, pastors, and tutors taught the rising generation how to read, write, and cipher and how to think and reason using the Bible as their primer or first book of instruction. In these 200 years, America produced five generations of extraordinary men and women who laid the foundation for a nation dedicated to the Christian principle of liberty and the art of self-government.

> The private system of education in which our forefathers were educated included home, school, church, voluntary associations such as library companies and philosophical societies, circulating libraries, apprenticeships, and private study. It was a system supported primarily by private benefactors, although there was a veneer of government involvement in some colonies, such as in Puritan Massachusetts. All was done without compulsion.[15]

The Old Deluder's Law of 1642 was passed in the Massachusetts colony. It stated, "All youth are be taught to read perfectly the English tongue, have knowledge in the laws and be taught some orthodox catechism." Colonial America also had dame schools, in which neighborhood children were taught to read and write by women in their own kitchens.

Unlike modern America, in which the most influential voice in the culture is the media, *in colonial America the pulpit served as the single most powerful voice to inspire the thinking and reasoning of the colonists.* What fired the colonial pulpit was the influence of the Reformers John Knox and John Calvin. Their teachings on the kingdom of Christ and the authority of the Scripture gave rise to the colonial form of self- and civil government.

The colonial pulpit, which began with men like Joseph Cotton, 1630 Puritan pastor of Boston, remained for 150 years the primary educational influence for the colonials through the preaching of such clergymen as Cotton Mather, Jonathan Edwards (evangelical patriarch), George Whitefield (First Great Awakening), Dr. John Witherspoon (signer of the Declaration of Independence), Samuel Davies (pastor of Patrick Henry), Jonas Clark (Lexington, 1775), and Peter Muhlenburg ("Give 'em Watts, boys!"), to name just a few. These were giants indeed, men who faithfully led their congregations to think biblically. Some clergy even donned the garb of a soldier during the American Revolution to fight tirelessly with pen and sword for the cause of Christian civilization on the North American continent. According to Yale historian Harry S. Stout,

> Over the span of the colonial era, American ministers delivered approximately eight million sermons, each lasting one to one-and-a-half hours. The average 70-year-old colonial churchgoer would have listened to some 7,000 sermons in his or her lifetime, totaling nearly 10,000 hours of concentrated listening. This is the number of classroom hours it would take to receive ten separate undergraduate degrees in a modern university, without ever repeating the same course![16]

The sermon provided colonial families an excellent educational experience. Sunday morning was not only a time to hear the latest news and see old friends, but it was also an opportunity to sit under a man of God who had spent many hours preparing for a two, three, or even four-hour sermon. Many a colonial pastor spent eight to twelve hours *daily* studying, praying over, and writing his sermon. Unlike sermons on the frontier in the mid-nineteenth century, colonial sermons were filled with the fruits of years of study. They were geared not only to the emotions and will, but also to the intellect.

The sermon was one of the chief literary genres in colonial America. Listeners followed sermons closely, made mental notes, and discussed the message with their family on Sunday afternoon. Thus, without ever attending a college or seminary, a churchgoer in colonial America could gain an intimate knowledge of Bible doctrine, church history, and classical literature. Questions raised by the sermon could be answered by the pastor or by books in church libraries that sprang up all over the colonies. Often sermons were published, and listeners could review what they had heard on Sunday morning. They were often passed from family to family in a community, as fathers sat nightly with their families around the fireplace rereading the scriptural references aloud and reviewing each principle with their children. Parents and pastors took seriously their role to educate both the head and the heart.

Sermons were also delivered on various public occasions, such as days of thanksgiving or fasting and the election of officers of the local militia. *They were often printed as political pamphlets, as pastors in the seventeenth and eighteenth centuries delivered dissertations on civil government.* "The annual 'Election Sermon'—a perpetual memorial that continued down through the generations from century to century—still bears witness [1860] that our forefathers ever began their civil year and its responsibilities with an appeal to Heaven, and recognized Christian morality as the only basis of good laws."[17]

The years 1740 to 1790 marked an age of "mighty men of God!"—an era of remarkable patriot-preachers who, by their faithful preaching and their righteous lifestyle, laid the foundation for the American Revolution and the founding of the new Republic. "To the Puritan pulpit we owe the force that won our independence."[18] England's King George III referred to the Revolution as the "Parson's Rebellion."

George Bancroft, nineteenth-century statesman and historian, wrote that "the Revolution of 1776, so far as it was affected by religion, was a Presbyterian measure. It was the natural outgrowth of the principles which the Presbyterianism of the Old World planted in her sons in the New World—the English Puritans, the Scottish Covenanters, the French Huguenots, the Dutch Calvinists, and the Presbyterians of Ulster [Ireland]. . . . The American Revolution was but the application of the principles of the Reformation to civil government."[19]

Presbyterian Scotsman Dr. John Witherspoon was president of the College of New Jersey (now Princeton University) and was especially prominent in the independence movement. His influence as a pastor/educator was enormous. One crown official in the colonies wrote back to England that the labors of such clergymen as John Witherspoon so influenced the shape of the conflict that it had very much become a religious war. Witherspoon tutored James Madison, architect of the Constitution and U.S. President; Vice President Aaron Burr; nine cabinet officers; twenty-one U.S. Senators; thirty-nine Congressmen; three Supreme Court justices; twelve state governors; and numerous ministers, lawyers, judges, and other public officials. Five of the fifty-five members of the Constitutional Convention were his students. He nurtured a whole generation of statesmen with the Scriptures and the Covenanters' view of civil government. He was elected as a delegate from New Jersey to the Continental Congress and served for five years. He was the only clergyman to sign the Declaration of Independence, and during his period in Congress he served on over 120 committees. "One realizes after seeing the character of these men why it is said that the colonists treated them with the kind of reverential regard that they refused to give kings and Anglican bishops."[20]

The true alliance between politics and religion is the lesson that was inculcated by the colonial clergy. "The pulpit of the Revolution is the voice of the Founding Fathers of the Republic, enforced by their example. They invoked God in their civil assemblies, called upon their chosen teachers of religion for counsel from the Bible, and recognized its precepts as the law of public conduct."[21] They prepared the new nation for the struggle for liberty with the Word of God and a deep trust in Him in their hearts. This was the colonials' source of moral energy.

The results of colonial education are most impressive. America's educational institutions—family, church, and school—produced generations of articulate, Christian men and women who could discourse on complex issues of self- and civil government. Samuel Adams, colonial patriot and father of the American Revolution, summarized the ideal of American colonial education: "To develop a wise and virtuous man, fit to be trusted with the liberty of his country."[22]

Teach Character and Understanding at Home

The first sphere of government in colonial America was the home. Home is where the foundation of character is laid and where self-government should first be learned and practiced. Man's capacity to govern himself is in direct proportion to his relationship with Jesus Christ and obedience to His Word. Childhood is the optimum time to receive Christ as Savior and when the principles of Christianity are most effectually impressed upon the mind. Much of human character and felicity depends upon the education of the young mind for both the development of its faculties and the application of truth to choices and decisions.

It was in the colonial home that fathers and mothers taught and modeled Christian character and established home habits of civility, morality, frugality, perseverance in well doing, self-governance, and the love of learning. The Bible was their primer for character education and the Book from which they taught their children how to read and reason with truth. Reverend Phillips, writing in 1869, described the role of the colonial American home with regard to forming the character and conscience necessary for Christian civil governance:

> The Christian home has its influence also upon the state. It forms the citizen, lays the foundation for civil and political character. . . . We owe to the family, therefore, what we are as a nation as well as individuals. The principle of home government is love—love ruling according to law. It is similar in its fundamentals to the government of the state and the church. It involves the legislative, judicial, and executive functions; its elements are law, authority, obedience, and penalties. The basis of its laws is the Word of God.[23]

John Adams, second President of the United States, and his wife Abigail were careful parents. They lived on a farm in Braintree, Massachusetts, and contributed significantly to the founding and constitutional eras of the United States. They left us a remarkable record through their lifetime correspondence of over 1,100 letters. Abigail was the daughter of a colonial New England pastor. She was home-educated and spent hours reading the books in her father's library. She, in turn, home-educated their five children. Their first son, John Quincy, served America for more than fifty years. He accepted his first diplomatic appointment at the age of fourteen as secretary to the U.S. minister to Russia. His first instruction was in the Word of God. So well did young Johnny commit the Word to his heart and mind that it became for him both compass and anchor in his long life of public service.

Johnny was a patriot by the age of seven. While his father served as a statesman in Philadelphia, he watched his mother melt her pewter utensils to make bullets for the Continental soldiers. He served his mother on their Braintree farm, and at the age of ten held a post-riding job delivering mail. It was at this age that John Quincy began his habit of writing. He is known for his personal diary that he maintained all his life, which comprises over fifty volumes.

His father, John Adams, never abdicated his responsibility to educate his children, even though he spent long months and even years away from New England in service to the new nation. In a 1778 letter to Abigail, he penned,

> Education makes a greater difference between man and man, than nature has made between man and brute. The virtues and powers to which men may be trained by early education and constant discipline are truly sublime and astonishing. . . . It should be your care therefore, and mine, to elevate the minds of our children, and exalt their courage, to accelerate and ani-

> mate their industry and activity, to excite in them an habitual contempt of meanness, abhorrence of injustice and inhumanity, and an ambition to excel in every capacity, faculty, and virtue. If we suffer their minds to grovel and creep in infancy, they will grovel and creep all their lives.[24]

Ten years at home, under his beloved mother's tutelage, was all young Johnny would have. At the age of eleven, he traveled to France with his father to serve him in his diplomatic role. However, Abigail continued her education of Johnny through her letters. A portion of a 1778 letter exhorts,

> Improve your understanding by acquiring useful knowledge and virtue, such as will render you an ornament to society, an honor to your country, and a blessing to your parents. Great learning and superior abilities, should you ever possess them, will be of little value and small estimation, unless virtue, honor, truth, and integrity are added to them. Adhere to those religious sentiments and principles which were early instilled into your mind, and remember, that you are accountable to your Maker for all your words and actions.[25]

As a young adult, John Quincy served as a diplomat in various European nations, as Secretary of State for President Monroe, and as a Congressman from Massachusetts. He was then elected the sixth President of the United States. After his four-year term as president, Adams returned home and ran for a seat in Congress. He is one of only two presidents to continue public service after his term in office, which he did for 18 years until his death.[26] He made many contributions as a legislator, not the least of which was his stand against slavery.

In 1811, John Quincy revealed his concern for the character of the next generation. He wrote a series of letters to his own son at boarding school on "The Bible and Its Teachings." A portion of one of these letters follows:

> I advise you, my son, in whatever you read, and most of all in reading the Bible, to remember that it is for the purpose of making you wiser and more virtuous. I have myself, for many years, made it a practice to read through the Bible once every year. I have always endeavored to read it with the same spirit and temper of mind, which I now recommend to you: that I,

> with the intention and desire that it may contribute to my advancement in wisdom and virtue. . . . My custom is, to read four or five chapters every morning, immediately after rising from my bed. It employs about an hour of my time, and seems to me the most suitable manner of beginning the day. . . .
>
> You have already come to that age to know the difference between right and wrong, and you know some of your duties, and the obligations you are under, to become acquainted with them all. It is in the Bible, you must learn them, and from the Bible how to practice them. Those duties are to God, to your fellow-creatures, and to yourself. "Thou shalt love the Lord thy God, with all thy heart, and with all they soul, and with all thy mind, and with all thy strength, and thy neighbor as thyself." . . .
>
> You will perceive that I have spoken of duties to yourself, distinct from those to God and to your fellow-creatures; while Jesus Christ speaks only of two commandments. The reason is, because Christ, and the commandments repeated by him, consider self-love as so implanted in the heart of every man by the law of his nature, that it requires no commandment to establish its influence over the heart; and so great do they know its power to be, that they demand no other measure for the love of our neighbor, than that which they know we shall have for ourselves as well as to them, and they are all to be learned in equal perfection by our searching the Scriptures.[27]

Colonial education successfully equipped five generations to think and reason justly with the revelation of God's Word for application in every sphere of life. It produced the Christian character and conscience required for governing the world's first Christian constitutional republic.

In the next chapter, Indian philosopher, theologian, and social activist Vishal Mangalwadi explains what happened when the Judeo-Christian framework and the Bible itself were jettisoned from the center of personal and national life in the United States, to be replaced by an alternative integration point, human beings, and an alternative worldview, the Atheistic/Darwinian worldview that became the framework for all of life. The whole of the country was deconstructed, and Christianity lost America.

FOUR

Seminary: Education or Religious Schooling?

Vishal Mangalwadi

In order to bless India, the pioneers of the modern missionary movement did  not establish a Bible seminary/institute or school. Instead, these Calvinist-Baptists founded Serampore College in 1818. Their leader, William Carey, was one of the greatest Bible translators/publishers of all times. Yet, along with teaching the Bible, that cobbler-turned-linguist taught botany, horticulture, astronomy, forestry, and agriculture. He founded India's Agri-Horticultural Society, built up India's second-best botanical garden in Serampore College, published scientific books, and pioneered Indian journalism. The college rapidly grew to become Serampore University in 1827.

Later, the Serampore University Senate handed over the departments of liberal arts and science to the secular government and confined itself to teaching theology. Did the university's theology unwittingly and fatally separate the so-called "sacred" subject of divinity from "secular" studies? This chapter is a big-picture critique of the modern movement of theological seminaries/Bible institutes/Bible schools.

Troubling Questions

William Carey's generation triggered India's renaissance. Has our fragmented worldview made theological education relevant for heaven but irrelevant for earth?

As of today, one cannot find a single copy of Sam Higginbottom's book, *The Gospel and the Plow* (1921),[1] in the library of the Sam Higginbottom Institute of Agriculture, Technology and Sciences. Is it because our theological education has no genuine interest in integrating theology with the "plow"? That is, with the science, sociology, economics, law, politics, and technology needed to bless India?

Why did twentieth-century theology cease making the church the light of the world? Did the corruption of Western theology inflict this disease upon India?

More importantly, is this separation of theology from the rest of the academy responsible for marginalizing Christianity in the world's premier Protestant nation—the United States of America?

Why Christianity Lost America

"Liberal theology" has self-destructed. From the outset, the idea was foolish that the Bible is humanity's Word, not God's, yet human reason can systematize the "science of God" (theology). Today, hardly anyone studies liberal theology to try to know God. Therefore, in this chapter, the "Bible Institute/School/Seminary" movement generally means evangelical, theological institutions. The theological ethos that established these institutions was radically different from the worldview of the Puritans who founded Harvard (1636), Yale (1701), and Princeton (1746). These universities were created to train men and women to serve the church and the world that God loves.

According to its motto adopted in 1692, America's first college, Harvard, was started by Puritans for "Christ and the Church" (*Christo et Ecclesiae*). Harvard, which arguably wrote America's DNA, is still the world's number one university. It continues to shape America. Christianity lost America for several reasons, principally because it gave up its best Christian colleges and retreated into the Bible seminary movement.

The Heart of the Matter: University versus Seminary

Harvard's iconic crest was adopted in December 1643. It made the pursuit of truth (*veritas* in Latin) the purpose of the university's existence, because God wants "all people to be saved and to come to the knowledge of the truth" (1 Timothy 2:4).

How do we discover truth? The Harvard Crest inscribed *veritas* on three books: (1) God's words, (2) God's works, and (3) God's reason, reflected in His image—man.

In order to discover truth, a student had to study all three and connect the dots discovered through them. The Bible institute/seminary movement departed from this wholistic epistemology in an attempt to derive truth exclusively from the Scriptures—the book of God's words.

The immediate intellectual force behind the Harvard crest was John Amos Comenius (1592–1670), the last bishop of The Unity of the Brethren church. His ninety books on education made him the father of modern education. He also helped shape the modern Protestant theology of "Nation" that forged the 1648 "Peace of Westphalia."

That theology created nations such as the United States of America and India.

Samuel Hartlib and John Milton invited Comenius to England in the early 1640s to launch what would have been the world's first "modern" college in Chelsea, London. The Civil War prevented the establishment of that college, but two significant things came out of his time in London:

- Comenius laid the intellectual foundations of the Royal Society. A majority (62 percent) of its founders were Puritans. At that time Thomas Hobbes was the only atheist thinker in England, and that disqualified him to be a member of history's most influential scientific society.
- New England's Governor John Winthrop interacted with Comenius and brought his philosophy of Christian education to America.

Besides Comenius, Christian thinkers who shaped Harvard's educational philosophy included Francis Bacon (1561–1626), Alexander Richardson (d. in or before 1629), William Ames (1576–1633), and Johann Heinrich Alsted (1588–1638). They believed that truth is known through rational revelation.

Martin Luther was an Augustinian monk and a professor at Wittenberg University. For a thousand years, his theological tradition had believed that in order to know truth one had to study God's two books: the book of God's words and the book of God's reason, reflected in His image—the human mind. The first book (Scripture) is understood through the second (reason).

Luther's iconic declaration at the Diet of Worms in 1522 articulated this worldview:

> Unless I am convicted by Scripture and plain reason I do not accept the authority of popes and councils, for they have

> contradicted each other. My conscience is captive to the Word of God. I cannot and I will not recant anything, for to go against conscience is neither right nor safe. Here I stand, I cannot do otherwise. God help me. Amen.[2]

The Book of God's Words—*Scripture*

Jesus confirmed the Old Testament view that truth and falsehood are both communicated in words and that God's Word is a source of our knowledge of truth.

- The Sidonian widow of Zarephath said to Elijah, "Now I know that you are a man of God, and that the word of the LORD in your mouth is truth" (1 Kings 17:24).
- The Lord Jesus said, "Your word is truth" (John 17:17); "Scripture cannot be broken" (John 10:35); "If you abide in my word, . . . you will know the truth" (John 8:31–32), etc.
- The apostles reinforced the Lord's teaching:
    - » Paul affirmed, "All Scripture is breathed out by God (2 Timothy 3:16).
    - » Peter taught, "No prophecy was ever produced by the will of man, but men spoke from God as they were carried along by the Holy Spirit" (2 Peter 1:21).

The Book of God's Reason

Luther taught Aristotle to his students and considered parts of the Greek philosopher's writings to be a corrupting influence upon Europe's intellectual life. Yet Luther—one of history's most important champions of God's Word—agreed with Aristotle that learning truth requires studying and using reason, including logic and mathematics. This aspect of medieval education came via Augustine, who considered reason to be God's distinctive gift to man. That is why Augustinian tradition believes that the mind must be developed, just as we multiply other talents given to us.

Augustine's theology of reason was grounded in the apostle John, who presented God as a rational person. For very good reason, Reformed theologian Gordon Clark translated John 1:1 as "In the beginning was reason [*logos*, word], reason was with God, and reason was God."[3]

What makes *word* different from *mantra*? A *word* is a sound with *sense*. A proposition makes sense only *because* it is a logical arrangement of words and sentences.

Many Bible schools no longer teach logic. Traditionally, however, theo*logy* required the study of logic. Timothy's pastoral role required him to *study* to show himself approved unto God, *one who exegetes the word logically* (2 Timothy 2:15).

Paul did not ask Timothy to memorize his words, for the Judeo-Christian Scriptures are not *mantras* to be memorized and enunciated correctly. God's Word is His wisdom. Therefore, Paul commands Timothy to "think over" his words (2 Timothy 2:7). To do theology is to think and interpret revealed data logically. It calls one to cultivate a logical mind.

The Book of God's Works

William Carey taught astronomy and botany. Sam Higginbottom taught agriculture, science, and technology because by their time Protestant theology had improved upon Luther. Luther studied the books of God's words and reason, but these could not teach him the truth about the solar system. In his usual bombastic style, Luther (1483–1546) wrote a pamphlet denouncing Copernicus's (1473–1543) theory that the earth revolves around the sun, not the sun around the earth. Soon afterward, Galileo's (1564–1642) careful observations of God's works—the actual motions of the planets—confirmed Copernicus's theoretical model.

Galileo took pains to exegete the Bible and argue that his sun-centered view of the solar system was consistent with the Bible. Yet his discovery challenged Luther's epistemology as much as it challenged the Pope's infallibility. Protestants and Catholics had to come to terms with the fact that it was not enough to study God's Word and reason. God asks us to study his works also. That study is necessary for us to rule over the earth (Psalm 8:6; 64:9; 72:12; 92:5, etc.). It was Francis Bacon (1561–1626)—often called the father of modern science—who forcefully championed the necessity of studying God's *works*.

The Scriptures say that "the heavens declare the glory of God" (Psalm 19:1a). In Romans 1:19–20, Paul says that God's works reveal the truth about God and His attributes, including His power, wisdom, and glory (see also John 9:3; 11:40).

Bacon's exposition of the Bible was the reason Cambridge University inscribed Psalm 111:2 at the entrance of Cavendish Laboratory—history's first scientific lab: "Great are the works of the Lord, studied by all who delight in them." The psalm celebrates God's work, both in nature and in culture. The Old and New Testaments record God's works so that we might study them in our quest for truth and then teach them to others. God's works reveal His love as much as His words do. That is why the church established research universities.

Christian scholars researched all three books of God: the book of God's words; the book of God's works; and the book of God's reason (including logic and mathematics) because, as Bacon reminded Christian scholars, God *reveals* as well as *conceals* truth. "It is the glory of God to conceal things, but the glory of kings is to search things out" (Proverbs 25:2). The rising and setting sun conceals the fact that day and night are caused by the earth's revolution, not the sun's.

Evangelicalism was America's dominant force during much of the twentieth century. Yet it did not build a single research university during its heyday. Why? One reason was its truncated epistemology that in order to know truth Christians should study only the Scriptures. Another factor was the belief that *revelation* means that God is in the business of revealing, not concealing matters. Research universities and labs were built on the knowledge that God's words and works conceal matters; we are endowed with reason in order to discover
 hidden treasures.

Fragmentation of Knowledge: From Modernism to Postmodernism

Medieval as well as modern universities saw theology as the queen of all sciences. When Isaac Newton (1642–1726/7) came to Cambridge, there was no department of science. What we call science was, for Newton, a study of the book of God's works. It was called Natural Philosophy, meaning wisdom and revelation concealed in God's creation but available to all.

The current fragmentation of knowledge began when Europe's Protestant philosophers surrendered to a Roman Catholic heresy that gave to the book of reason the controlling authority over the books of God's words and works. Reason is necessary to understand Scripture, nature, and culture. However, reason's job is to understand, receive, interpret, synthesize, apply, and articulate revelation, not to judge it.

Enlightenment rationalism began as a Roman Catholic heresy. Catholic theology affirmed the ultimate authority of the Scriptures and the Church. The Church's interpretation of the Scriptures claimed infallibility. It did not grant final authority to individual reason because it believed in original sin. Therefore, it was not traditional Catholicism but a heresy to think that Adam and Eve's "fall" affected the heart but not the mind. Therefore, the mind (reason, logic) could discover truth without grace, without revelation or inspiration.

René Descartes's rationalism ignored total depravity and exalted the book of reason above the books of God's words and works: this was the beginning of humanist hubris. For revelation is the only reason a section of the Roman Catholic Church had trusted reason. The Orthodox Church failed to develop universities because it did not fully embrace Augustine's biblical perspective on human reason as God's image.

The Protestant Reformers were theologians. Through thinkers such as Luther and Calvin, Protestantism inherited the best of Catholic thought. European thinkers built upon that foundation. Tragically, however, some of their European followers, mainstream Protestant philosophers, theologians, and apologists, surrendered to rationalist arrogance. They, too, put reason above revelation and undermined the authority of Scriptures, of *Logos* (Word become flesh), and quickly of reason itself.

Modernism failed to give us the knowledge of truth because it destroyed revelation—the only available ground of our confidence in reason. Its overconfidence in reason quickly degenerated into skepticism, ignorance, unbelief, immorality, and defiance of God's authority. Western rationalism (including theological "modernism" or liberalism) undermined confidence in the Scriptures because it was oblivious to the fact that it was sawing off the very branch upon which it sat. That, however, was a lesser tragedy.

More disastrous was Christian "fundamentalist" (i.e., evangelical) reaction to "liberal" modernism. During the twentieth century it abandoned the university in favor of Bible institutes/seminaries. Evangelicalism threw the baby out with the bathwater. In reacting against rationalism, fundamentalism abandoned studying the books of God's works and reason. The Reformers' slogan, *Sola Scriptura* (Scriptures alone), began to be misunderstood to mean "Study only the Scriptures." A theologian may learn Greek, but he does so to study the Bible, not Plato.

Why Seminaries Plunged Universities into Intellectual-Moral Darkness

In 1944, the Socratic Club in Oxford invited C. S. Lewis to speak on the theme "Is Theology Poetry?" No one writes theology in verse. So, the question was not whether theology should be classified as poetry. The issue was whether Christians believe the creeds because those propositions are true or because they satisfy poetic imagination.

Lewis concluded his magnificent speech with a statement that has become classic: "I believe in Christianity as I believe in the rising sun. Not simply because I see the sun, but because through it I see everything else." Lewis's argument was that theology is the university's queen of sciences because the Bible is the sun that gives light to every branch of inquiry. God's Word gives confidence in (humble) reason. Together, the Scriptures and reason make sense of everything else. That epistemology of rational revelation enabled the university to develop a coherent "world and life view." Without the Bible, the university is without a central or common source of light (a sun) through which each department can comprehend its subject and connect it with other branches of knowledge and with life outside the academy.

Postmodernism completed the fragmentation or *silofication* of knowledge. Without the sun, without revelation, it had to discard the very notion of truth—*veritas*. Education ceased being the pursuit of truth. It became merely the acquisition of information, skills, and degrees in the quest for employment and power (sometimes, mainly an opportunity for sports, fun, and networking). This turned every university faculty into a silo. Deprived of the sun, every silo had to invent its own light, which took the form of a distinct vocabulary, creeds, and initiation rituals that could not be questioned by novices or noninitiates. The Bible seminary started the problem. Two illustrations may help bring clarity:

Can God turn water into wine in an instant? Could He have made Eve a fully grown woman at the moment of her creation? If so, He can also create in an instant a fully developed universe. But did He? How is that question to be investigated? A young-earth creationist may maintain that, about four thousand years before Christ, God created the universe in six days, each of twenty-four hours. Did he arrive at that conclusion because he carefully synthesized all the information gleaned from the books of God's Word, works, and reason? Or does he hold his belief as a dogma, because he believes that we know truth by reading only the Scriptures? Is it biblical to not study God's works (science) objectively?

Why does an evolutionist believe that a professor of law, logic, or mathematics cannot understand or question the evidence for macroevolution? It is because evolution—a great theory—has become a dogma. Evolutionists do not allow nonspecialists to scrutinize their dogma because postmodern biology, geology, and paleontology are silos—dogmatic, occult sciences accessible only to the initiated, not to outsiders.

Why Is the Postmodern University Sinking into Intellectual and Moral Darkness?

The sad answer is that the Bible institute/school/seminary movement put the university's sun—the Bible—into an academic silo. Instead of seeking truth by synthesizing knowledge revealed in the books of God's words, works, and reason, the Bible seminary isolated God's words from his works and reason. Silofication of the sun pushed other departments into darkness.

The Gospel and Plough School of Theology is uniquely placed to begin reversing the destructive epistemology of previous centuries. GPST can chart a new path for global theology if it takes seriously the vice chancellor's call to equip and enable theology students to go to other departments to study books of God's works and reason. Likewise, the theology faculty must equip itself to welcome students of agriculture, science, technology, and the humanities to take courses in the book of God's words. The day must come when professors of physics, anthropology, and medicine will pursue postdoctoral research in theology, not to become pastors but in order to synthesize information gleaned from God's three books.

Too much of today's discussion of education focuses on the programmatic and policy level of education; it focuses on the what and how of education, as well as the latest educational techniques and technologies. In the next chapter we will focus on the most basic, most unasked, and most important question: Why Education?

Vishal Mangalwadi, who wrote Chapter Four, is described by *Christianity Today* as "India's foremost Christian intellectual."[4] He is an international lecturer, social reformer, political columnist, and the author of 14 books. Born and raised in India, Dr. Mangalwadi studied philosophy at several universities, at L'Abri Fellowship in Switzerland, and in Hindu ashrams.

In 1976 Vishal turned down several job offers in the West to return to India, where he and his wife, Ruth, founded a community to serve the rural poor. Their efforts to transform rural India resulted in violent opposition, several arrests, and the razing of their home and community. Vishal continued to work for the empowerment and liberation of peasants and the lower castes at the national headquarters of two political parties. His firsthand experience of social evils motivated him to study how the West became a relatively just, free, and prosperous civilization. *Truth and Transformation* is one of several results of that study.

In 2003 William Carey International University honored Vishal's life, service, and books with a Doctor of Laws degree. Vishal and Ruth have two daughters and five grandchildren.

Among his many books are *This Book Changed Everything—Volume I: The Bible's Amazing Impact on Our World* (2019); *The Book that Made Your World: How the Bible Created the Soul of Western Civilization* (2011); *Truth and Transformation: A Manifesto for Ailing Nations* (2009); *Corruption versus True Spirituality—with Francis Schaeffer* (1998); *India: The Grand Experiment* (1997); *Missionary Conspiracy: Letters to a Postmodern*

Hindu (1996); *What Liberates a Woman? The Story of Pandita Ramabai: A Builder of Modern India—with Nicol McNicol* (1996); and *The Legacy of William Carey: A Model for the Transformation of a Culture—with Ruth Mangalwadi* (1993).

Bibliography

On Sam Higginbottom:

Hess, Gary R. 1967. *Sam Higginbottom of Allahabad: Pioneer of Point Four to India*. Charlottesville: The University Press of Virginia.

Higginbottom, Sam. 1921. *The Gospel and the Plow: Or, The Old Gospel and Modern Farming in Ancient India*. New York: The Macmillan Company.

———. 1949. *Sam Higginbottom, Farmer: An Autobiography*. New York: Charles Scribner's Sons.

On William Carey:

Mangalwadi, Vishal, and Ruth Mangalwadi. 1999. *The Legacy of William Carey: A Model for the Transformation of a Culture*. Mussoorie, UA: Good Books.

On Why Christianity Lost America:

Grant, Edward. 2001. *God and Reason in the Middle Ages*. Cambridge University Press.

Marseden, George M. 2006. *Fundamentalism and American Culture*. Oxford University Press.

Noll, Mark A. 1994. *The Scandal of the Evangelical Mind*. Grand Rapids: Eerdmans.

On the Place of Reason in Christian Education:

Cochrane, Charles Norris. 1940. *Christianity and Classical Culture*. Oxford University Press.

Scott, David Hill. "A Vision of Veritas: What Christian Scholarship Can Learn from the Puritan's [*sic*] 'Technology' of Integrating Truth," *LeadershipU*, *leaderu.com/aip/docs/scott.html*.

On Biblical Theology and the Making of the Modern World:

Mangalwadi, Vishal. 2011. *The Book That Made Your World: How the Bible Created the Soul of Western Civilization*. Nashville: Thomas Nelson.

FIVE

Why Education? The Lost Purpose for Learning

Christian Overman

Followers of Christ in the United States[1] are coming to the sober realization SG-5a that the biblical foundations for law, civil government, economics, family, and gender that once provided commonly accepted harbor lights for society have been replaced. An incessant move toward the secularization of society and the privatization of Christianity that took place in the twentieth century was enormously successful, being expedited greatly through elementary and secondary schools.

The shaping of nations begins in the minds of children. Nation-shaping ideas acquired in elementary and secondary schools are not immediately felt on a national level because it takes time for little acorns to grow into giant oaks. But grow they will. And, as has been said many times, "Ideas have consequences."

This chapter is a call to action for those who plant nation-shaping ideas into young minds, by design or by default: *elementary and secondary educators*. This includes school teachers and headmasters, Sunday school workers, and other church personnel who interact with students between the ages of four and eighteen. This also includes parents, who educate their children daily by default or design, and it includes pastors, who educate from the pulpit.

It's time to restore the lost purpose for learning. This purpose has been neglected for 150 years in the U.S. and begs to be revived, both in the U.S. and elsewhere in the world. This can be done if we will first understand what has been lost, and then take the necessary steps to restore the lost purpose in ways that are *systemic*, *intentional*, and *repeatable*.

This will not be a quick and easy fix. But we must begin by making modifications in thousands of schools and churches without further delay.

Albert Einstein once said, "The formulation of a problem is often more essential than its solution." With this in mind, let's start by formulating the problem, to more fully understand what has been lost before we look at how it can be regained.

Can Secularized Schools Be Neutral?

U.S. schools prior to the twentieth century were predominantly Christian in orientation and practice. This is evidenced by the common practice of teacher-led Bible reading and prayer, as well as the academic texts that were used, containing much Scripture and references to Jesus Christ, sin, and salvation. These texts included *The American Spelling Book* by Noah Webster (1822), considered the standard spelling book in U.S. schools; *The National Reader* (1828); *A Common-School Grammar of The English Language* (1871); and the popular *McGuffey Readers*, which sold at least 120 million copies between 1836 and 1960.[2]

Perhaps the most noteworthy evidence of Christian thought being overtly mixed with education in the U.S. prior to the twentieth century is found in Noah Webster's *American Dictionary of the English Language* (1828). This magnum opus took Webster 28 years to complete. It is full of scriptural references in his definitions of words, as this "Father of American Scholarship and Education" standardized the English language for all U.S. citizens. Webster was also one of the Founding Fathers of the United States.

As the United States transitioned from nonregulated Christian schools to a centralized state school system in the late 1800s, Princeton theologian A. A. Hodge wrote, "It is self-evident that on this scheme, if it is consistently and persistently carried out in all parts of the country, the United States system of national popular education will be the most efficient and wide instrument for the propagation of atheism which the world has ever seen."[3]

My only comment about Hodge's statement (besides applause for his recognition of the danger of civil government ruling over schools) is that the situation today has gone far beyond atheism.

Some will balk at Hodge's words, insisting that state education is neutral when it comes to matters of faith. But this question of not mixing faith with education must be carefully examined. The question is not whether faith *will* be allowed to mix with education, but *which faith* will be mixed? The fact is that faith is being mixed with state schools today on a daily basis. It's just a different *kind* of faith than the one that was commonly mixed with United States schools for some 300 years following the Reformation.

In state-run schools of the U.S. today, it is no longer permitted to teach students that God speaks to humanity through the Bible. It is no longer permitted to teach students that the Bible provides a standard for social and moral order. Yet it *is* allowable to teach that social and moral order is "clarified" by society itself, or by individuals within that society (including oneself).

So, here's the big question: *If it is a religious matter to teach—or to imply—that the Bible provides a standard for social and moral order, is it not also a religious matter to teach—or to imply—that it does not?*

If it is a religious position to say, "Jesus is Lord of all, and by Him and through Him all things exist," is it not also a religious position to say—in so many words, or lack thereof—"Christ and the Bible are irrelevant to our discussion of biology, physics, and math"? Are not *both* statements religious statements?

To teach students that Christ and the Bible are irrelevant to biology, physics, and math can be done very effectively without telling them this directly. A teacher does not have to stand in front of a class and say "the Bible has nothing to do with our discussion" to communicate the message that the Book is irrelevant.

If we think the current U.S. system of education is religiously neutral, we must think again. If state schools were indoctrinating children in Buddhism, Islam, or Native American animism, many Christian parents would hit the ceiling. Maybe. But when it comes to the indoctrination of children in John Dewey's so-called "Common Faith," which he referred to as a *nontheistic faith*, Christian parents are curiously passive.[4]

Apparently enough Christian parents think that secularism is "neutral" and that if their children can learn to read and write well enough to enter a university they'll give secularized education a pass. Apparently enough Christian parents feel that if teachers don't stand up in front of a class and say, "The Bible is a fairy tale," things are okay. Yet when teachers don't place a single academic subject into the context of a biblical frame of reference over a period of 13 to 14 years, are those teachers really being "neutral"?[5]

My biggest concern about young Christians being indoctrinated by secularized schools, however, is *not* that they will become *atheists*. My biggest concern is that they will become *dualists*. A dualist is one who reads the Bible, prays, goes to church on Sunday, and yet doesn't make any significant connection between God's Word and what goes on in the Monday through Friday workplace because they think "faith" is a personal, private matter, while the workplace is public, and therefore "secular."

Dualists see the Bible as relevant to personal life, or to the affairs of the church, but not relevant to what goes on in the Monday-through-Friday workplace. Dualists don't mix the biblical worldview with driving a truck, painting a house, or managing a bank, because they didn't mix it with geography, literature, or sports. Why mix the Bible with life in the city? Building houses, selling vegetables, and practicing law are all "secular" endeavors, aren't they? But where exactly *is* this "secular" world?

The SSD Infection

Many Christians view life as having two bifurcated compartments, somewhat like this:

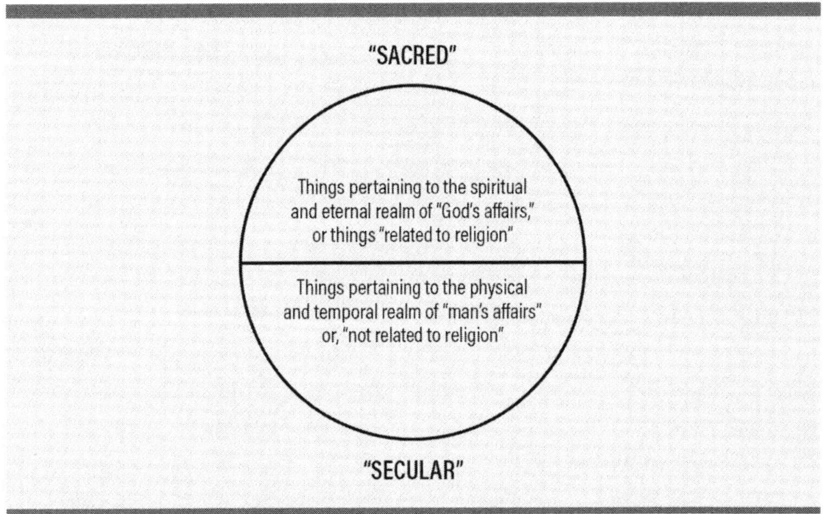

A dualist lives life as though there is a sacred-secular divide (SSD). The "sacred" things of life include Sunday morning worship, Bible study, prayer, witnessing, and going on mission trips. These are the things that have *real* significance because they *truly* matter to God. These things have to do with the "things above," which we should be setting our minds upon. These are things related to the spiritual side of reality that last forever.

The so-called "secular" things don't have as much significance because they don't last. They are not eternal. The "secular" things include mowing the lawn and earning money to keep a roof overhead and pay the electric bill. These things are necessary, but not as important to God. They fall under the category of "the things of earth." These are things that are supposed to grow "strangely dim" as we focus on Christ. Right?

Let me suggest a more biblical way of looking at things:

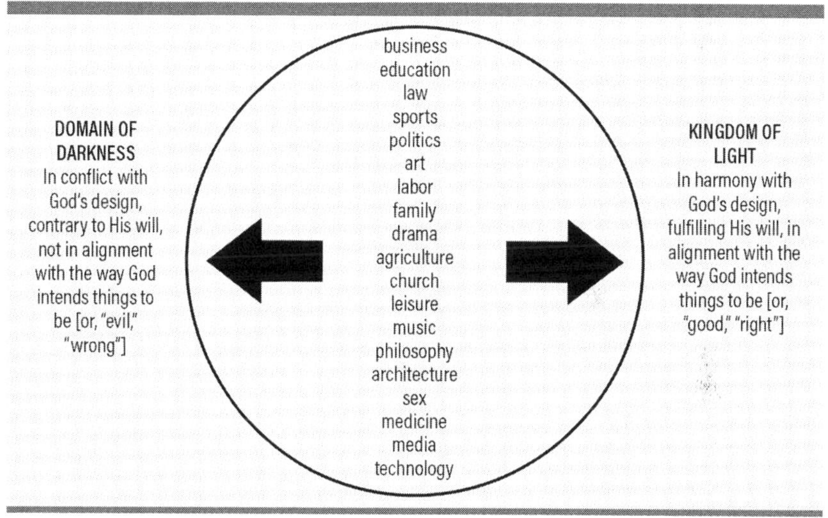

In this view of things, *any* sphere of human endeavor may be engaged in *harmony* with God or in *conflict* with Him, in *alignment* with God or in *opposition* to Him.[6] We can live as God intended, with the overall well-being and wholeness that come only from living in harmony with God and His purposes (*shalom*), or we can live cross-current to His intentions. The contrast here is between light and darkness, good and evil, right and wrong, in *any* sphere of life.

Of course, not all things in a fallen world can be called "sacred." Some things are profane, being far out of sync with the Creator and His intentions. But as the poet Wendell Barry put it, "There are no sacred and unsacred places; there are only sacred and desecrated places."[7]

Regardless of the current condition of the world, and the state of things within it, Christ is Lord *of all* (Acts 10:36), and therefore His authority is boundless and borderless. As I wrote in *Assumptions That Affect Our Lives*, "[S]ince there is nothing which stands outside of God's authority, He is as relevant to what goes on in civil government as He is to the way business functions, to the way family members relate to one another . . . to the way a local church functions. In short, He is Lord of all, and no less relevant to one area of human endeavor than another."[8]

After a 13- to 14-year dose of secularism in early education through secondary school (even inadvertently by Christian teachers who would never speak badly of the Bible, yet must remain silent about its role in seeing how every academic subject fits into the big picture of reality), students will most likely come out the other end as dyed-in-the-wool dualists who think the Bible is relevant to church life and personal piety but not relevant to business, law, or politics, because it wasn't relevant to history, algebra, or soccer. This is a problem.

And it isn't just a problem in schools. It's a problem in churches as well. Dualism hinders the church from helping people to make real connections between the so-called "secular" world (where most of us spend most of our time), and the intentions of God for the here and now. As Dorothy Sayers in her essay "Why Work?" expressed it,

> In nothing has the Church so lost Her hold on reality as in Her failure to understand and respect the secular vocation. She has allowed work and religion to become separate departments, and is astonished to find that, as a result, the secular work of the world is turned to purely selfish and destructive ends, and that the greater part of the world's intelligent workers have become irreligious, or at least, uninterested in religion.

Sayers went on to say, "But is it astonishing? How can anyone remain interested in a religion which seems to have no concern with nine-tenths of his life?"[9]

Are Christian Schools Contributing to the Problem?

During my 14 years as a Christian school principal, I hired a good number of teachers. They were all born-again believers, dedicated to the Lord and to the profession of teaching. Yet few came to my school with any understanding of how their classroom instruction would either *promote* or *dispel* SSD, the sacred-secular divide. For the most part, awareness of the issue was off the radar. Regrettably, the reason many Christian school teachers are unaware of this issue is that they have not been made aware of it through the teacher training programs of universities today—even the so-called "Christian" universities.

Usually SSD is passed on unknowingly and unintentionally, like a virus.[10] A Christian school can have great chapel speakers, mission trips, an inspiring "Spiritual Emphasis Week," and solid Bible classes, but if the academic instruction that goes on in science and math, as well as the skill development that takes place in music and sports, and the textbooks that are used, do not "connect the dots" between whatever the students are learning and the bigger picture of God's intentions for those subjects and skills, dualism will be propagated by default.

If I were considering a Christian school for our four children today, I would do well to do some homework before enrolling them, by asking the headmaster, "What specific training have your teachers received for designing lesson plans that will help my children see God's purpose and intentions for whatever it is your teachers are teaching?"

You can be certain that more than 95 percent of the teachers in most Christian schools were not trained to do this in their education courses at the university.

Based on how the headmaster answered the above question, I would do well to interview three teachers, asking them the following question: "In the past two weeks, what have you specifically said or done during your instructional time that would help my son or daughter to understand God's purpose and intentions for what you're teaching?"

If three Christian school teachers could show me a specific lesson plan they used in the past two weeks that helped their students to see how what they are learning fits into God's purpose and intentions for that subject, I would advise parents to enroll their children without delay and tell their friends. A great treasure has been found.

When it comes to the matter of textbooks used in Christian schools, the worldview of the writers will come through by design or default, whether through what is *stated* in the text or through what is *not* stated. Here again, there is no neutral ground. The religion of the writers cannot be divorced from the text, and this includes religion of the nontheistic type, which dominates the secularized texts of our day.

Textbooks carry as much weight as teachers—or more. Adolf Hitler understood this when he declared, "Let me control the textbooks and I will control the state."[11] The same Christian schools that will not hire non-Christian teachers may think nothing of using textbooks that work in the opposite direction. This is a violation of good educational sense. And dualism will continue to be propagated if textbooks do not present subject matter in the context of a wholistic biblical worldview that connects that subject matter with God's purpose for the subject itself.[12]

Many Christian parents who attended dualistic schools (whether the state-school type or the private-school type) don't see a problem with sending their children to dualistic schools, because *they* (as parents) "turned out okay."

But my question is: *Did* they?

Did we?

To one degree or another we have all been infected by SSD. But whether a person *realizes* she has been infected with SSD is quite another matter, and this is what makes SSD so difficult to cure. Whereas atheism is easy to spot, dualism is much more subtle, like an unrealized parasite in the gut. While atheism is

viewed by Christians as the enemy, dualism is our unrealized bedfellow.

The Lost Idea of "The Whole"

Let me present my case, starting with the disappearance of "wholism." I'm starting here because to understand the bane of dualism we must first understand the wane of wholism.

No less than 100 years after A. A. Hodge's prophetic statement, Allan Bloom wrote *The Closing of the American Mind.* Bloom taught at Cornell University, the University of Toronto, Yale University, and the University of Chicago. Bloom was not a Christian.[13] Yet in his book Bloom observed the following:

> In the United States, practically speaking, the Bible was the only common culture, one that united the simple and the sophisticated, rich and poor, young and old, and—as the very model for a vision of the order of the whole of things, as well as the key to the rest of Western art, the greatest works of which were in one way or another responsive to the Bible—provided access to the seriousness of books. With its gradual and inevitable disappearance, the very idea of such a total book is disappearing. And fathers and mothers have lost the idea that the highest aspiration they might have for their children is for them to be wise—as priests, prophets or philosophers are wise. Specialized competence and success are all that they can imagine. Contrary to what is commonly thought, without the book even the idea of the whole is lost.[14]

I would be hard pressed to come up with one paragraph that explains the problem better than this one. We have lost the very *idea* of the *whole* of things. As Bloom observed, with the disappearance of the "total book" (the Bible), *the idea of the whole* is lost. Dualism and the resultant privatization of Christianity and secularization of society are the natural consequences of this loss.

It may be hard for some to believe, but in the United States prior to 1962 Bible reading was commonly practiced in state schools. How did this come about? Partly because Noah Webster (1758–1843), the Founding Father who started the first daily newspaper in the U.S. and was called the "Schoolmaster of the Nation," held that "any system of education . . . which limits instruction to the arts and sciences, and rejects the aids of religion in forming the character of citizens, is essentially defective." When Webster wrote "religion," he had Christianity in mind. In the same letter, he wrote, "No truth is more evident to my mind than that the Christian religion must be the basis of any government intended to secure the rights and privileges of a free people."[15] Webster also declared the Bible to be "that book which the benevolent Creator has furnished for the express purpose of guiding human reason in the path of safety, and the only book which can remedy, or essentially mitigate, the evils of a licentious world."[16]

While one may question Allan Bloom's assertion that it was "inevitable" that the biblical vision of the order of the whole of things would disappear from the public square, the fact is that it *has*. Today it is confined to the four walls of certain churches, and to the private lives of certain individuals.

Why does this matter? *Because we are all affected by its loss.* In recent years, some U.S. citizens have been shooting bystanders in shopping malls, strangers in movie theaters, and little children in classrooms. Policemen have been ambushed on the streets. Retirement savings of thousands have vanished because of toxic schemes developed by smart graduates of Ivy League schools. Local school boards have required the full spectrum of LGBTQ demands to be adopted as district-wide policy, so schoolboys who "self-identify" as girls are now allowed to use the girls' shower rooms. Men who self-identify as women are allowed to use women's facilities outside of the schoolhouse. Have we lost our sanity? At the very least, we are a "troubled" nation. And deeply divided. Could this possibly be related to the loss of a biblical vision for "the order of the whole of things?"

There I go again, talking about the negative effects of dualism! But, before I proceed, let me say a word about its spelling.

Not long ago, I received an e-mail from someone informing me that the word *wholistic* is not spelled with a *w*. In the past, I was informed incessantly of this by my computer spellchecker, too. But I fixed this pesky problem by adding *wholistic* to my computer's dictionary. So, now it is spelled with a *w*. Credit for its coining goes to Darrow Miller and Bob Moffitt, co-founders of Disciple Nations Alliance. In Miller's book, *LifeWork*, he writes: "Wholism speaks of the whole of God's Word to the whole man in the whole world. We [Miller and Moffitt] recognize that *wholism* is a coined word. But we prefer it to the word more commonly used, *holism*, which has been co-opted by the New Age movement."[17] I'm following suit.

Let me expound a bit on the biblical basis for wholism. I am turning to the Scriptures because, like Webster, I accept them as the Word of God and the never-changing plumb line for True Truth. Upon that premise this entire chapter rests.

God Made All Things, Owns All Things, and Upholds All Things

The simple yet profound starting point for wholism is God's creation of the entire material and spiritual realm. Without Him, *nothing would exist*. But since I think most people reading this chapter accept this premise, I will not dwell on it here. Suffice it to say, "In the beginning, God created the heavens and the earth" (Genesis 1:1). The universe is no accident. The earth and all it contains did not come into being through a series of random, unplanned "happenings."

Yet one thing that is not often discussed is God's ongoing *ownership* of all things, even after the entrance of sin into the world. The significance of this cannot be overstated. That's because if we get the issue of ownership wrong, it makes a huge difference in the way we view the world.

My mentor, Dr. Albert E. Greene Jr., touched upon this problem when he wrote, "There is a subtle derailment which often occurs in Christian thought at the point of the Fall. We tend to think that when man sinned, God simply relinquished the whole creation as a botched job and left Satan to do what he wanted with it. Nothing could be further from the truth."[18]

The world and all it contains are as much God's stuff *after* the fall as they were *before* the fall. The fall did not change God's ownership status. He not only made it all in the beginning and continues to hold it all together—He *owns* it all, and this has enormous ramifications for human beings. When we mow the lawn, we're cutting *His* grass. When we pound a nail, it's *His* metal we're pounding. When we examine a drop of water under a microscope, it's *His* creation we're looking at. He is speaking to us through what we observe every day.[19]

Planet Earth, and all it contains, do not belong to Satan. The Scriptures plainly tell us, "The earth is the LORD's and the fullness thereof, the world and those who dwell therein" (Psalm 24:1). As Abraham Kuyper, founder of the Free University of Amsterdam and former Prime Minister of the Netherlands, famously put it, "There is not a square inch in the whole domain of our human existence over which Christ, who is Sovereign over all, does not cry, Mine!"[20]

Although the devil may act as though he owns the place, he does not. He never created anything in his life. He only distorts and destroys what God has made. In Luke 4:5–6, when Satan offered Jesus "all the kingdoms of the world" in exchange for worshipping him, was this a legitimate offer? Consider the source.[21] More on this later.

Hebrews 1:3 tells us that Christ is upholding all things by the word of His power. *All things!* The seen and the unseen, the temporal and the eternal, the material as well as the spiritual are continually upheld by Him. Creation (a much better word to use than "nature") originally came into being through the premeditated act of God. Yet the very fact that all of creation *continues* to exist today is as much a wonder as its first appearance!

It is not as though God made it all at some point gone by, and now it functions quite well all on its own, running according to so-called "natural" laws. Look out your window once again. The present is as magnificent as the beginning; the very continuing existence of the universe is as awesome as its first appearance. Christ perpetuates the whole through the ongoing "word-deed" (Hebrew: *dabhar*) of His voice.

Dr. Erik Strandness, author of *The Director's Cut*,[22] has made the astute observation that we might better describe the universe as created not *ex nihilo* (that is, out of nothing) but *ex cōgitātiō* (out of thought). Dr. Strandness points out that creation is knowable only because it came out of God's *thought*, not out of *nothing*. Thought speaks to thought. And through His creation the Creator speaks. Every day. Every hour. To all generations, in every part of the planet. As the psalmist wrote in Psalm 19:2–4a, "Day to day pours out speech, and night to night reveals knowledge. There is no speech, nor are there words, whose voice is not heard. Their voice goes out through all the earth, and their words to the end of the world."

The fact is that, if it were not for the continuing, supernatural, creation-sustaining "voice" of the Almighty God holding it all together, "nature" would be no more. In terms of how most people think about the "natural" and the "supernatural," the "natural" has come to mean "the normal operation of a self-governing system," while the "supernatural" refers to "the interference of God in that system." Yet Colossians 1:16–17 tells us, "For by him [Christ] *all* things were created, in heaven and on earth, visible and invisible, whether thrones or dominions or rulers or authorities—all things were created through him and for him. And he is before *all* things, and *in him all things hold together*" (emphasis added).

God Created Humans with a Specific Role and Function in Mind

In Genesis 1:26–28, we see exactly what God had in mind for human beings when He created Adam and Eve. Let me say that again, so you can savor the full weight of what Genesis 1:26–28 is actually telling us: *We see the specific role and function God had in mind for humans when He created us.*

What *role* did God have in mind for humans before He made Adam and Eve? What *purpose* did He have in mind for us? What *intention* was behind His creation of human beings? Specifically, God had *governance of His creation* in mind when He said, "Let us make man in our image, after our likeness. *And let them have dominion . . . over all the earth*" (emphasis added.)

Albert Wolters, in his essay "The Foundational Command: 'Subdue the Earth,'"[23] says that it is "almost impossible to overemphasize the importance of this first and fundamental command of God to humans." Wolters calls it "the first and fundamental law of history." This first mention of purpose, which Wolters says "all subsequent revelation presupposes," is often called "the cultural mandate." I simply call it "the First Commission."

Wolters further notes that "man is to be fruitful *in order to* multiply, he must multiply *in order to* fill the earth, and he must fill the earth *in order to* subdue it." And then he adds that we were created in God's likeness and image *in order that we may fulfill this command.*

Psalm 115:16 says, "The heavens are the LORD's heavens, but the earth he has given to the children of man." *The Message* puts it this way: "The heaven of heavens is for God, but he put us in charge of the earth."

Stop and think deeply about this. *We were created to govern over the Blue Planet and everything in it.* This includes water (both salty and fresh varieties); air; electricity; sound waves; light; lead; uranium; silver; rubber; maple trees; money; fish; birds; cows; carrots; copper; fingers; thumbs; arms; feet; real estate; sweet potatoes; soybeans and every derivative thereof, including plastic and dyes (thank you, Dr. George Washington Carver); as well as digital images, smart phones, e-books, ships, cars, airplanes, glue, paper, antifreeze, pencils, ice cream, and cake!

Humans were made to rule over whole *systems*, too, because without *systems* governance over things cannot take place: Civil systems, legal systems, and economic systems are all required. But let me be very clear here. I am not suggesting some sort of political rule by the church over the State. Christ's second coming will address this matter. Nor am I suggesting that some sort of Christian "Sharia Law" be imposed, or that Christians take exclusive control of all cultural institutions.[24] Nevertheless, as individual followers of Christ, we are all to "occupy" until He comes again. This certainly includes bringing the rule of God to bear in our various occupations as we live out the implications of our faith in the context of our daily work, whether it be in the home or in the public square.

God clearly created human beings with the intention that we govern over all He created and sustains (see Psalm 8). This necessitates economists, judges, and legislators. God's overarching purpose for human beings to govern well over *all things* provides extraordinary purpose for education and remarkable incentive for learning.

Work worth doing is *any* expenditure of energy, mental or physical, for pay or not, that rightly manages God's stuff and brings glory to Him by employing one's God-given gifts and abilities for the benefit of others—or prepares one to do so. SG-5c

There's No Room on Christ's Throne for Two

When I say Satan doesn't own Planet Earth or anything in it, some might be thinking, "Satan may not *own* it, but he sure does *run* it!" But what does Satan "run"?

Yes, in John 14:30 Jesus refers to Satan as "the ruler of this world." And in 1 John 5:19 we read that "the whole world lies in the power of the evil one." But what "world" is the Scripture talking about here?

The English word *world*, translated from the Greek word *kosmos*, has several different meanings in Scripture, depending on the context. It can mean: (1) *the physical realm of creation*, as in Romans 1:20 ("For his invisible attributes, namely, his eternal power and divine nature, have been clearly perceived, ever since the creation of the world, in the things that have been made") or (2) *populated regions*, as in Romans 1:8 ("[Y]our faith is proclaimed in all the world [*kosmos*]") or (3) *the human race in general*, as in John 1:29 ("Behold! The Lamb of God, who takes away the sin of the world [*kosmos*]!).

But *kosmos* ("world") may also refer to *a system of thought and behavior that runs contrary to the will and ways of God*. We see this in 1 John 2:15–16: "Do not love the world [*kosmos*] or the things of the world [*kosmos*]. If anyone loves the world [*kosmos*], the love of the Father is not in him. For all that is in the world [*kosmos*]—the desires of the flesh and the desires of the eyes and the pride of life—is not from the Father but is from the world [*kosmos*]." Here John defines the "world" as a system of thought and action governed by the lust of the flesh, the lust of the eyes, and the pride of life. It is *this* "world" we are not to love. It is *this* "world" that Jesus was not "of" (John 8:23); it is *this* "world" His followers are also not to be "of" (John 17:14–16), and it is *this* "world" Satan rules. This is different from the "world" God so loved, as proclaimed in John 3:16. These are different meanings of the word "world." Clearly, if one verse tells us to "love not the world, and another that "God so loved the world," we must conclude that there is a difference of meaning in the word "world."

Satan is not the king of Planet Earth. Yes, he is the ruler of the *world system* that runs contrary to the will and ways of God. As mentioned above, I suspect Satan's brazen offer to Christ on the mountaintop (Luke 4:5–7), to give Him all the kingdoms of the world if He would only bow down and worship him, was outlandishly bold and bogus. Lucifer acts as though he owns Planet Earth, but there is only one Owner and only one King. His name is Jesus. Satan is indeed the "prince of the power of the air" (Ephesians 2:2), but this prince is no king. There is no room on the throne for two. Christ's authority rests over the *whole* of heaven *and* earth, right now. If we get this wrong, dualism comes easily.

Christ's rule is over *all*. The King's domain (that is, His *king-dom*) knows no boundaries. Christ is Lord of all, all the time, everywhere, both in heaven and on earth concurrently, right now (Acts 10:36). But does this mean that everything happening on Planet Earth is His will?

When I hear Christians say "God is in control," I have to ask myself what is really meant by this statement. Do we mean to say that God *causes* everything to happen that happens on Planet Earth? Is *everything* that happens God's will? I can't read my Bible and draw this conclusion. Why would Jesus teach us to pray to the Father, "Thy will be done on earth as it is in heaven," if His will were already being done?

So, how do we reconcile the all-encompassing, here-and-now rule of God with all the ungodly things happening on Planet Earth every day? And why is there so much suffering in this world if God is continuously sustaining all things? If He owns it, why does He allow things to go on that are painful or evil?

This answer may not satisfy everyone, but it works for me: God is in absolute control, but He does not control all things absolutely.

What does this mean? It means that God has the power and authority to do whatever He pleases, whenever He wants. If He desires, He can make a donkey talk. He can make an ax head float. He can turn bullets into bubbles. But the God of the Bible does not control all things absolutely all the time. Gravity works the same on all of us, and it is not suspended when a Christian steps off a cliff. People are not puppets on God's strings. We can violate His will, and we do. At times we act in ways God doesn't want us to act. This is what *sin* is about.

Yet, while we have the *ability* to violate God's authority, we were never given the *right* to do so. When humans disregard God and act contrary to His will, we dare not say, "God is in control." Yet when humans act contrary to God's will, this does not negate the fact that Christ is still Lord of all, all the time, everywhere. In *this* sense, He is "in total control." We don't *make* Christ Lord; He *is* Lord! It's our place to *recognize* His authority, accept, and embrace it.

Yet even if people don't embrace it, Christ's authority still applies to everyone, all the time, everywhere. His authority is all-inclusive and nonselective. It applies as much to our personal life as to our public life. It applies as much to what goes on in church as it does to what goes on in civil realms. It applies as much to what goes on in our families as it does to what goes on in our workplaces. It applies as much to non-Christians as to Christians. The biblical injunctions against theft, murder, and adultery (Matthew 19:16–19) are not for believers only.

Jesus is Lord of all, whether or not people submit to Him as such. Even the demons know there is only one God, and they tremble (James 2:19)! If *they* know this, we can be sure their *boss* knows this, too.

The authority of Christ is over the *whole* of humanity. There is no public/private split, no Christian/non-Christian distinction when it comes to the *jurisdiction* of Christ's authority. No human can "impose" it on anybody. It simply *is*. Like gravity.

"Secondary Creations" Glorify God When Well Done

We live in *God's* world, even in its fallen, broken condition. It is God's creation that we're surrounded by, and it is God's stuff we're taking into our hands when we form and shape anything. He not only created it out of His thought in the beginning, but He owns it and sustains it all now. And He commissioned us to manage *all* of it, even in its fallen and broken condition. We are to "tend and keep," as only God's image-bearers can.

As His designated Earth-tenders, we are designed to make "secondary creations" out of God's "primary creation," even if what we create doesn't last past Wednesday. A good chef creates works of culinary art that may not last more than a few hours. This glorifies God *innately,* because a good meal is the outworking of the chef's image-bearingness, whether the chef realizes it or not. The chef is a "secondary creator," ruling well over salmon, rice pilaf, and bleu cheese.

And through this act of imitation, God is glorified. Even if the chef doesn't realize it.

In using the term "secondary creation," I do not mean to imply that creations made by human beings are "second rate." I simply mean to say they are made *out of* God's primary materials. God initiated all things, and humans made in His likeness and image "create" things out of something first materialized by God. We *make something of it.* And I believe God delights in seeing us do this.

As His designated Earth-tenders, we fulfill God's intention for us to govern over all things when we mow the lawn, cut hair, fix automobiles, and negotiate the sale of a house. We fulfill God's intention for us when we create good legislation, play a violin, or write a book, ruling well over words, sounds, and ideas. It is our great honor to govern over His stuff. And through our imitation, when our "secondary creations" align well with God's nature and character, He is glorified.

This applies to *all* legitimate forms of work, whether it's making cars, light bulbs, or computers. Whether it's building roads, skyscrapers, or furniture. Filling cavities. Washing clothes. Feeding the family . . . and the dog. Governing well over *all* things to the glory of God is our calling and honor as His designated Earth-rulers.

If we think Planet Earth is "God's creation now disowned" and we see Satan as "king of the planet," then we may see our sole purpose on Planet Earth as telling others how they can go to heaven when they die. I am not minimizing the importance of evangelism. But when we see the *whole* of God's domain "in the light of His glory and grace," as the song puts it, the things of Earth do *not* grow "strangely dim." Quite the opposite.

When we view the Earth as "God's good creation now broken" and we understand our God-given role and assignment in it, then the gospel truly is more than the Gospel of our Personal Salvation. It is the gospel *of the kingdom* (the King's domain), which, in fact, is the term used in the Bible to identify the gospel itself. Yes, it is Good News that my soul is saved from hell. But that's not *all* there is to the Good News. The Good News *of the kingdom* is that Christ restores *things* as well as *souls*. What kind of "things?" Earth things!

I'm not remotely suggesting that all things will be fully restored before Christ comes again. But it is clear from Scripture that the "ministry of reconciliation," that Christ gave us in this present life (2 Corinthians 5:18; see verses 17–20) is not limited to human souls (Colossians 1:16–20). His King-domain is not limited to "spiritual things." *His King-domain is as broad as creation is wide.* The scope of Christ's reconciliation extends to the *whole of creation*, which goes far beyond the human soul. The scope of His redemption extends to all that was affected by the fall, and this is all of creation.

Colossians 1:16–20 says,

> For by him all things were created, in heaven and on earth, visible and invisible, whether thrones or dominions or rulers or authorities—all things were created through him and for him. And he is before all things, and in him all things hold together. And he is the head of the body, the church. He is the beginning, the firstborn from the dead, that in everything he might be preeminent. For in him all the fullness of God was pleased to dwell, and through him to reconcile to himself all things, whether on earth or in heaven, making peace by the blood of his cross.

To reconcile all *things*? Business things? Artistic things? Civil things? Yes, "that in *everything he might be preeminent*." God's scope of reconciliation includes not only *people* but *things*. Things *on earth!*

The ideas I am writing about here are not new. Following the reformational work of Martin Luther and John Calvin, early pioneers of what I call "wholistic education" such as John Amos Comenius (who was not only a world-class innovative educator but a bishop in the Moravian church), Johann Heinrich Alsted, William Ames, and Alexander Richardson developed approaches to learning that set a new course for human history.

Every U.S. citizen can be thankful for the biblically informed concepts these educational reformers developed, because the nation-shaping ideas they set into motion laid a foundation for something remarkable to follow, the likes of which the world had never seen, lasting for some 300 years.

One such history-shaping idea is called the "Puritan Circle of Knowledge," which went as follows:

1. God, the Prime Creator, **initiates** all things through His primary creation of everything:

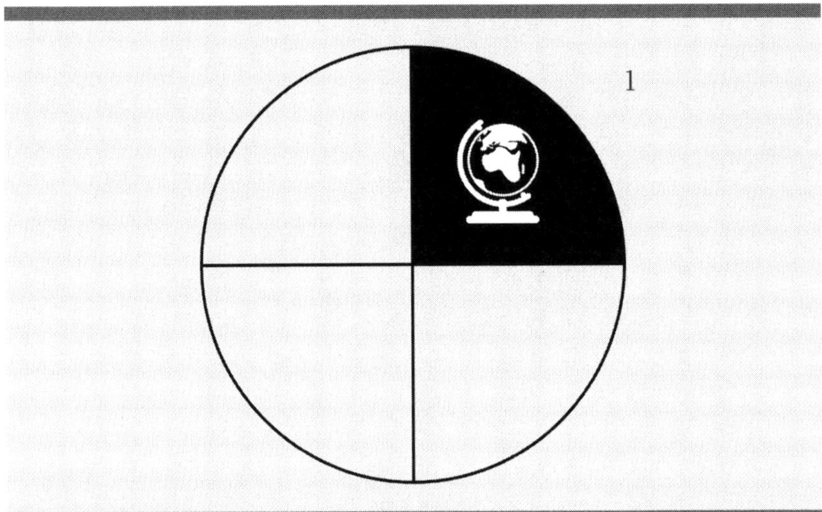

2. Humans **discover** what God has made, and this discovery is a big part of what education is about:

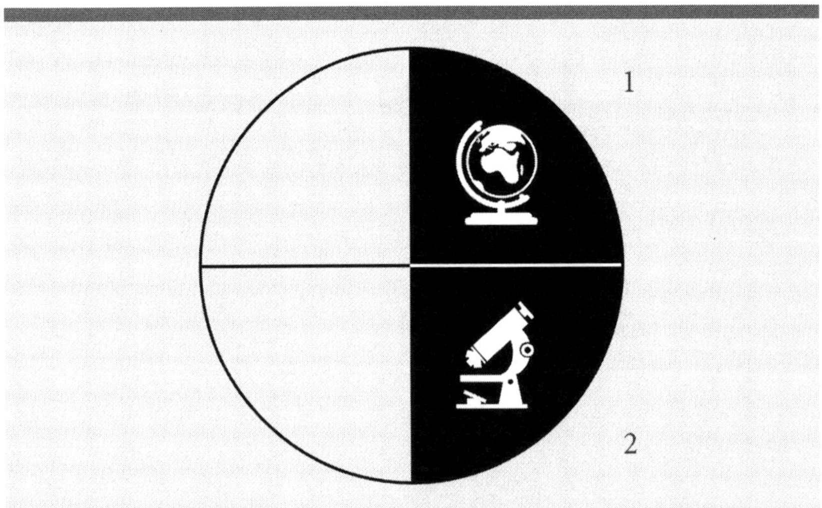

3. Humans **imitate** God by making "secondary creations" based upon their discovery and understanding of His primary creation:

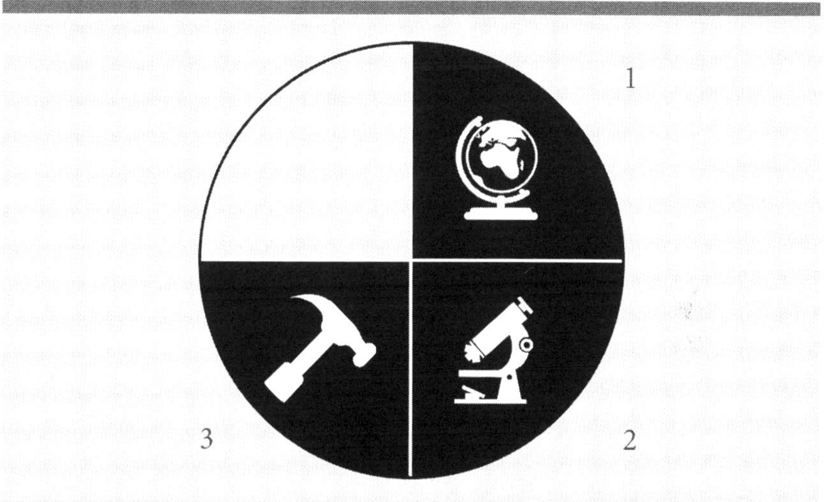

4. God is **glorified** through the imitation of Him in human occupations of all kinds:

So, the shoemaker *imitates God* by making beautiful and functional "secondary creations" out of God's primary creation. The shoes serve the needs of people and glorify the Prime Creator *through the imitation of Him*, thus bringing glory full circle from God back to God through vocation. The furniture maker *imitates God* by making beautiful and functional "secondary creations" out of God's primary creation. The furniture serves the needs of people and glorifies the Prime Creator *through the imitation of Him*, thus bringing glory from God back to God through vocation. The banker, the lawyer, and the businessman each glorifies God by serving the financial needs of people, bringing justice to the world, and creating employment for the community through *the imitation of God via their respective occupations*. And in so doing, God is glorified and communities are able to flourish.

Dr. David Scott notes, "The emphasis on use [in the Circle of Knowledge] fit[s] in nicely with the practicality of the Puritan mind, providing a philosophical foundation for the working vocations. . . . The human being as an artisan can follow in the footsteps of the Divine Artist. Through this circular pattern of the created order, humanity can fulfill its cultural mandate (Genesis 1:26–28) and returns glory back to God."[25]

I have no doubt this is why the Puritan pastor George Swinnock declared, "The pious tradesman will know that his shop as well as his chapel is holy ground."[26] Done in the right way, with the right attitude, for the right reasons, any "secondary creations" that imitate God well will glorify Him and bless humanity. This is true whether one is making shoes, running banks, or rearing children.

This understanding of "vocation" provided a backdrop for the early flourishing of the United States. To recover such ideas could change the course of history once again. As Gibbs and Morton put it, "Recovering this . . . would be like discovering a new continent or finding a new element."[27]

Ideas like the Puritan Circle of Knowledge provided purpose for education itself, just a few hundred years ago. John Milton, a Puritan leader, summed it up well when he wrote in his essay "Of Education," "The end [purpose] then of learning is to repair the ruins of our first parents by regaining to know God aright, and out of that knowledge to love him, to imitate him, to be like him, as we may the nearest by possessing our souls of true virtue."[28]

And in the same essay Milton wrote, "I call therefore a complete and generous education that which fits a man to perform justly, skillfully and magnanimously all the offices both private and public of peace and war."

It doesn't get more wholistic than that.

"Set Your Mind on Things Above"

But some followers of Christ may be thinking, "Doesn't Saint Paul say, 'Set your mind on things above, not on things on the earth'?" Indeed, Paul does. But let's take a close look at the context of that statement in the first 15 verses of Colossians 3:

> If then you have been raised with Christ, seek the things that are above, where Christ is, seated at the right hand of God. Set your minds on things that are above, not on things that are on earth. For you have died, and your life is hidden with Christ in God. When Christ who is your life appears, then you also will appear with him in glory.
>
> Put to death therefore what is earthly in you: sexual immorality, impurity, passion, evil desire, and covetousness, which is idolatry. On account of these the wrath of God is coming. In these you too once walked, when you were living in them. But now you must put them all away: anger, wrath, malice, slander, and obscene talk from your mouth. Do not lie to one another, seeing that you have put off the old self with its practices and have put on the new self, which is being renewed in knowledge after the image of its creator. Here there is not Greek and Jew, circumcised and uncircumcised, barbarian, Scythian, slave, free; but Christ is all, and in all.
>
> Put on then, as God's chosen ones, holy and beloved, compassionate hearts, kindness, humility, meekness, and patience, bearing with one another and, if one has a complaint against another, forgiving each other; as the Lord has forgiven you, so you also must forgive. And above all these put on love, which binds everything together in perfect harmony. And let the peace of Christ rule in your hearts, to which indeed you were called in one body. And be thankful.

When Paul says "seek the things that are *above*," the context makes it clear that he's talking about *tender mercies, kindness, humility, meekness, longsuffering, forgiveness, love, peace, and thankfulness*. These are the "things above." When Paul says to not set our mind on *earthly* things, he's not talking about hardwood floors, lawnmowers, and computers. He's not talking about banking, manufacturing, or civil service. He's talking about *fornication, uncleanness, passion, evil desire and covetousness, idolatry, anger, wrath, malice, blasphemy, filthy language, and lies*.

To interpret this as a directive to not engage with the material world runs counter to our designated role as Earth-tenders. Our unique calling as humans, to govern over the planet, doing His will on earth as it is in heaven, to be *in* the world but not *of* it, occupying until He comes again, requires all sorts of *work*. And education is essential to this end.

Some people may think that when Adam and Eve sinned, they forfeited their role as governors over the planet. They think that, like ambassadors caught in an act of treason, Adam and Eve were expelled from the garden and removed from their positions as God's vice-regents over the planet. In this scenario, Earth-ruling, or creation-tending, could no longer be the job description of human beings. If this is the case, then our work can no longer be a way of fulfilling the governmental function God had in mind when He created humans.

Yes, we are exiles and strangers in a fallen world. This has become increasingly evident to followers of Christ in the United States who are now needing a crash course on how to live as children of light in Babylon. We are out of sync with this present world system, because the fallen world isn't the way God originally made it to be. This present world system is alien to Him and to His ways, and at times it is hostile. The fact that all of creation is in need of restoration underscores the reality that the way things currently are is foreign to God's original design. That's why people experience toil and suffering in this life, and yes, that's why followers of Christ sometimes get beat up along the way (thrown to lions). Yes, we are out of sync with a world system that is increasingly hostile to the faith (see Hebrews 11), but we're in "the race set before us" nonetheless (see Hebrews 12), and the turf we're running on is God's field, even in its broken condition. There is no other place to run the race!

If we embrace the notion that our original job description, the first commission of Genesis 1:26–28, was rescinded at the fall, or assume that it doesn't apply to life in "Babylon," then we will have a very difficult time seeing how our shop, as well as our chapel, can be "holy ground." But God is the owner of every pair of shoes in every shoe store in the world. And He claims rights to every customer who walks through the doors. If this is true, then how can selling shoes be a "secular" job? It's all God's stuff. His leather. His laces. And He calls us to love our neighbors by imitating Him through the creation of good shoes

and selling them well.

Earth-Tending Is God's Assignment for Human Beings

Work, at its core, is an act of governance. Governance over wood, metal, cows, cotton, and carrots. Governance over sound waves, electrical currents, and wind.

Governance over computer keyboards, fiber optics, and digital images. Governance over people. Governance over things. Governance over ideas. Education that is truly wholistic will equip the next generation to engage in this task well.

During my years as a Christian school principal, I do not recall a single conversation with any of my peers as to how our schools might be more intentional about envisioning and equipping the next generation to govern well over all the planet through various occupations as God's appointed Earth-tenders. This overarching purpose for learning had disappeared from the conversation.

I was once speaking to a group of Christian school teachers and administrators at a conference hosted by the largest Christian school association in the world. The room fell breathlessly silent when I posed this basic question, "What is the purpose of education?"

Before anyone could reply, I answered my own question this way: "The purpose of education is to equip the next generation to govern well over this material world."

I let the silence hang. Then someone near the front broke the silence with, "Would you mind repeating that?"

I did. And then I asked whether anyone had ever told them this before. *Not a single hand was raised.*

Psalm 115:16 says it clearly: "The heavens are the LORD's heavens, but the earth he has given to the children of man." The Message puts it this way: "The heaven of heavens is for GOD, but he put us in charge of the earth." Yes, the earth is the Lord's and everything in it (Psalm 24:1), yet He has given humans charge of it, as His appointed vice-regents.

Wait! *Really?!* Who has charge of Planet Earth?

You and I do. And our neighbors. Think about it. Human beings were created for the express duty of governing over God's earth and everything in it.

If it is God's intention for human beings to govern this material world, shouldn't the purpose of education be to equip the next generation to do this well? *This* provides meaning for education—and purpose for teachers. Yet few Christian teachers have heard this.

Why?

I'll give you a hint: *How many sermons have you heard about God giving humans charge of Planet Earth?*

Earth-tending is God's clear intention for human beings, and it is an immense job! That's because the task of Earth-tending is as broad as creation is wide. It requires varied occupations, including carpentry, civil service, high-tech work, and homemaking. It involves physical work (as with Adam the landscaper, tending and keeping the garden) and mental work (as with Adam the zoologist, naming the animals). Both kinds of work occurred before the fall.

Work is not a curse! It is our great responsibility and privilege, as caretakers and shapers of God's creation. Our God is a working God, and we are made in His likeness and image *so that* we can carry out this function well. The curse pronounced by God after sin entered the world has made our work more difficult, for sure. Because of the curse, our work is often toilsome. But it was the *ground* that was cursed. Not work itself.

When pastors and missionaries are said to be in "full-time Christian service," and plumbers are said to be doing "secular work," the implication is clear: Plumbing is not full-time Christian service. It's not even *part-time* Christian service. But for the plumber who is a follower of Christ, isn't plumbing really full-time Christian service?

Does the Lord *care* about *plumbing* on Planet Earth? Does God want plumbing to be done well here? Isn't the plumber's ultimate employer the Lord, as Paul told the slaves in Colossians 3, exhorting them to do *whatever* they do "as unto Him" (in the very same chapter where Paul talked about not setting our minds on things of earth)? So, if Pete the plumber is working for the Lord, doing something God wants done in the earth, isn't Pete doing the "work of God"? This may sound like heresy to some. Most Christians would refer to plumbing as the "work of God" only if it were plumbing done through a missions organization. But, as Dorothy Sayers put it, "The only Christian work is good work well done."[29]

There is a common notion among Bible-believing Christians that if a person is *really* going to serve God, repairing a sewer system can't be compared with the work of a pastor or a missionary. The fact that we can even separate the two in our heads is indicative of the degree of our problem. Yet, as Ray Bakke, in *A Theology as Big as the City*, wrote, "Christians are the only people who can truly discuss the salvation of souls and the rebuilding of city sewer systems in the same sentence."[30] That is, we *ought* to be able to.

Most of us are products of education that reinforced the sacred-secular divide, whether in state schools or Christian schools. We are thinking dualistically when we don't view the two tasks of plumbing and preaching as a whole, or when we maximize personal evangelism while minimizing plumbing.

Yet the two endeavors are like two wings of an airplane. As my friend Dr. Al Erisman, author of *The Accidental Executive*[31] and former executive for the Boeing Company, put it, "Which wing is more important for flight, the left wing or the right wing?" To ask such a question is irrational.

Evangelism and good works are indeed "two wings of the same airplane." We are not saved *by* good works, but we *are* saved *for* good works. Ephesians 2:8–10 says, "For by grace you have been saved through faith. And this is not your own doing; it is the gift of God, *not a result of works*, so that no one may boast. For we are his workmanship, created in Christ Jesus *for good works*, which God prepared beforehand, that we should walk in them" (emphasis added). Should the good works God had in mind for us to do before He created Adam and Eve be limited to volunteer work at the mission or helping elderly widows buy groceries? Can the work of a plumber installing sinks and toilets come under the category of *good works for which he was created?* The fact that the plumber gets paid for it makes no difference. He *ought* to get paid for his work.

The sacred-secular divide runs deep. I remember telling my mother when I was about 12 years old that there were only two professions in life worth doing: being a pastor or a missionary. I recall my rationale for making this statement. It was the idea that saving souls is the *only* thing worth doing in this present life, because the soul is the only thing that lasts for eternity. The material world was destined for total obliteration, I thought. Eternity in heaven was all that mattered.

Yes, 2 Peter 3:10 tells us that both the earth and the works that are in it will be burned up. In this chapter, Peter points to the flood of Genesis as God's first great judgment by water. In that judgment, Peter tells us, the world was *destroyed* by water. Yet the earth was not washed away into nothingness. God's judgment by water was thorough, yet the earth passed through that judgment. The next great judgment will be by fire. Does this mean that the earth will become a "crisp job," reduced to ashes and nothingness? In that same chapter, Peter tells us that there will be a new earth (verse 13). God's judgment by fire will be a cleansing, purging fire, for sure. But we cannot conclude from 2 Peter 3 that God's judgment by fire will result in a *disappearance* of Planet Earth, any more than His first judgment by water did. The Bible speaks of a new earth with trees, jewels, and streets. There will be human beings there, with bodies. Revelation 21:24–26 speaks of the "kings of the earth" (earth rulers?) bringing "the glory and the honor of the nations" into the New Jerusalem. It appears that some "earthly" things will pass through God's judgment by fire. (This is a great mystery, and mysteries lend themselves to debate. I can't comprehend it all. I'll leave the details to God.)

As a boy in my church, when I sang song lyrics like "Turn your eyes upon Jesus . . . and the things of earth will grow strangely dim," I lumped business, school, and civil government into the "things of earth," along with everything else having to do with the material world.

One of the favorite songs of my church youth group was "I'll Fly Away": "Some glad morning, when this life is o're, I'll fly away. To that land on God's celestial shore, I'll fly away." Like a bird out of a cage. Heaven was the goal, and bringing others there with me was the sole reason for my living. That's what the Great Commission of Matthew 28 is all about. Right?

Because it is such an important issue, we need to take a closer look at that Great Commission of Matthew 28 and see how it relates to the First Commission of Genesis 1.

What Exactly Is the Great Commission?

Christ's last earthly command (Matthew 28:18–20) is more than a directive to produce converts. It is a directive to teach converts *to observe all things that He commanded.* Where is this observation to take place? I think it's safe to say that Christ had Planet Earth in mind, because He says, "I am with you always, to the end of the age." Presumably that's an earth age. Where is the observation of all Christ commanded to take place? In church? Yes. At home? Yes. In our personal lives? Yes. But what about life beyond the four walls of the church and the home, such as in the workplace, where we spend most of our waking hours?

Christians are already sprinkled like salt throughout the full spectrum of society *in the workplace*. It is here that we have prime opportunities to "observe all things that Christ commanded," living out the implications of Christ's commands in the context of our daily work. That is, in the context of customer service, marketing, salary and benefit issues, work conditions, decision-making policies, products, production, pricing, contracts, employee-employer relationships, co-worker relationships, hiring and firing policy, accounting, management, strategic planning, profit distribution, and community service. Does the gospel of the kingdom have anything to say about these things? Indeed, it does. While alignment with Christ's commands in some of these areas might mean getting fired, it isn't the same kind of "firing" some early Christians experienced in ancient Rome: being burned alive.

Most Christians in Rome, however, were not burned alive. They lived their daily lives in such a way that people were amazed at how they could approach the challenges of life so differently. Athenagoras described the Christians of Rome to Marcus Aurelius in this way:

> With us, on the contrary, you will find unlettered people, tradesmen and old women, who though unable to express in words the advantages of our teaching, demonstrate by acts the value of their principles. For they do not rehearse speeches, but evidence good deeds. When struck they do not strike back; when robbed, they do not sue; to those who ask, they give, and they love their neighbors as themselves. If we did not think that a God ruled over the human race, would we live in such purity? The idea is impossible. But since we are persuaded that we must give an account of all our life here to God who made us and the world, we adopt a temperate, generous, and despised way of life.[32]

The early followers of Christ lived out their faith in everyday life without fanfare. This included their work lives, as Athenagoras observed. They took Paul's exhortations to heart, as he wrote to believers in Thessalonica: "Aspire to live quietly, and to mind your own affairs, and to work with your hands, as we instructed you, so that you may walk properly before outsiders" (1 Thessalonians 4:11–12).

If today's Christians are unable to see the value of their work beyond feeding their families, finding opportunities to evangelize, or making money to support the work of pastors and missionaries (all valid things), we will miss one of our greatest opportunities to demonstrate the value of our principles to our fellow citizens in our present-day "Rome."

We glorify God on the earth by imitating Him well through our daily occupations. This is "theology of work" in a nutshell. What better opportunity to be *in* the world but not *of* the world system than in the nitty-gritty realities of our everyday work? As a byproduct, the world can be "turned upside down" again, as it was in Paul's day. We're overdue for another upside-down turning.

Are Christians called to change culture? Not by our own human strength, of course, or by the "arm of flesh" (2 Chronicles 32:8). But when we authentically live out our faith in the context of our whole lives, including our work lives, allowing the grace of Christ to be expressed through us, we *will* influence the surrounding culture. When we live out our faith in the world, by God's grace, this *will* have an effect upon others and on our environment. The results are up to God.

When, as the Great Commission requires, we teach converts to obey all that Christ commanded in the context of their private lives as well as in their public lives, they cannot help but "flavor" the surrounding culture. The history of Rome bears this out. This is what being salt and light is about. If the early Christians had privatized their faith, they would never have been thrown to lions.

All of life takes on new meaning when it is viewed in the context of a biblically informed frame of reference, a biblical worldview. Our call to steward the full spectrum of God's creation is not a matter of polishing brass on a sinking ship but of affirming God's good creation, broken by the fall and in need of governance by human beings who are imitating God in the office as well as in the shop.

The ramifications of all this for education are enormous! Education, then, becomes a matter of *envisioning and equipping the next generation to rule well over God's entire good-but-broken world, imitating Him well in the totality of the here and now, both in public and in private, through human occupations of all kinds, hence occupying until He comes again.*

This is the lost purpose for learning. The purpose it's time to restore.

Education Is for Earth-Tending

Let me recap the main points so far:

The responsible role of governance over Planet Earth was given to human beings (Genesis 1:26–28), created in the image and likeness of God so we can fulfill this role well. Planet Earth was not given over to Satan at the fall but remains God's full possession even in its broken condition (Psalm 24:1). Christ continues to hold all the atoms of the material world together "by the word of His power" (Hebrews 1:3), and Jesus's authority presently resides over all things, including all earth things, such as legal things, artistic things, agricultural things, industrial things, and civil things, being not limited to "spiritual things" and "church things" (Acts 10:36). God is now working in Planet Earth through His redeemed people to reconcile all things to Himself. This includes the human soul, as well as whole systems (2 Corinthians 5:17–20 and Colossians 1:16–20). When we imitate God well via "secondary creations," we bring glory full circle back to Him through occupations. Even in "Babylon." Or, perhaps I should say, *especially* in Babylon.

In recent years, the United States has transitioned from a post-Christian culture to an anti-Christian culture. Our challenge now is to authentically live out our faith in Babylon, while not "eating the king's meat." That is, we need a generation of Daniels, who know how to live and work *in* the world, while not being *of* it.

If this is true, then Dallas Willard was onto something when he wrote:

> There is truly no division between sacred and secular except what we have created. And that is why the division of the legitimate roles and functions of human life into the sacred and secular does incalculable damage to our individual lives and to the cause of Christ. Holy people must . . . take up holy orders in farming, industry, law, education, banking, and journalism with the same zeal previously given to evangelism or to pastor and missionary work.[33]

This gives no place to a sacred-secular divide that so many think is really there. We certainly *do* live in a secular*ized* world, where Christ is marginalized, ignored, or completely denied, but this is a fantasy world.

So, what is the purpose for learning? Again, it is so human beings may engage in governing well over the things of earth through meaningful occupations, imitating God by ruling well over the *whole* of creation, even in its broken condition. And again, I say, *especially* in its broken condition.

It's about bringing farming, business, law, economics, and journalism into alignment with the King, by God's grace, so that His will may be done on earth, as it is in heaven, as Jesus prayed. For students, it is about bringing finger painting, soccer, and essay writing into alignment with the King. And in so doing, Christ's King-domain "comes" to school.

Seeking first the King-domain of God, and understanding how Christ's King-domain connects with all that is studied in school, together constitute the best reason for education. This reason stands a chance of catching the imagination of students who are floundering in school, seeing little purpose for their studies, and having little incentive for learning. While they are really Earth-rulers on an assignment conceived by God before the first humans were created, most students don't realize this. Regrettably, most teachers don't realize this, either.

The Message translates Proverbs 29:18a this way: "If people can't see what God is doing, they stumble all over themselves." The King James version puts it this way: "Where there is no vision, the people perish." This includes students *and* teachers. Without *meaning*, most students just get by. And some not even that.

When it comes to school, there's no shortage of *what* to learn. The shortage is *why*. For many students, it's *meaning* that's missing. The kind of meaning that motivates. Beyond grades, future paychecks, and accolades.

As a young man in a Christian high school, I failed to see the bigger picture, and thus I could not connect God's purpose for my life with my daily schoolwork. I wanted to serve the Lord. But I thought that only pastors and missionaries did this. And later, I failed to make any connections between my selling of shoes (which I did as a college student) and the King-domain of God. That's because I equated the kingdom of God with church and church-related things. I did not see the King's domain as the *whole* of the material world. I did not understand that selling shoes was part of the kingdom of God.

What does selling shoes have to do with the kingdom of God? If we separate the two, we will never understand what the one has to do with the other. *Selling shoes is God's work, too.* This is an understanding we need to restore, and Christian education can play a major role in this restoration.

How? By seamlessly embedding biblical premises of work, economics, and human flourishing into the standard elementary and secondary curriculum in such a way that students are able to see how *whatever* it is they are studying fits into the context of something much larger.

What Is a Theology of Work, Economics, and Human Flourishing?

The term *human flourishing* here does not refer to some kind of prosperity gospel. It refers to an *abundant life* (as Jesus put it) with meaning, purpose, and hope, accompanied by a deep sense of satisfaction and completeness that can come only from living as God intended. It refers to overall well-being and wholeness, whether it's relational, economic, or otherwise, that come from being in unity with God and His purposes, living in alignment with the kingdom of light, where things are as they should be, not only for individuals but for nations. The biblical word for this is *shalom*.[34]

Space limitations do not allow me to elaborate here, but the following list will help introduce what I mean by "biblical premises of work, economics, and human flourishing." This list is a starting point, taken from a larger list of premises titled "99 Truths about Work, Economics and Human Flourishing," available at the Worldview Matters® website (*biblicalworldview.com/Godspleasure.html*).[35]

1. God is the first and finest worker. (Genesis 1:1,31)
2. God has continued to work even after His initial creation of all things. (John 5:17)

3. God owns all things—the material world is His "stuff." (Psalm 24:1)
4. God determined before the creation of Adam and Eve that humans would govern over (steward) all things on earth. (Genesis 1:26–28)
5. The material world has not been forsaken by God, in spite of the fall and the fact that His world is broken and in need of restoration. (Genesis 3:21; John 3:17; Colossians 1:19–20)
6. Pain and suffering are realities in a fallen world, but work itself is not a curse. (Romans 5:12; Ephesians 2:10)
7. Humans were created by God to work. (Genesis 1:26; 2:15)
8. Humans are God's workmanship, created for doing the good work He conceived of ahead of time for them to do, even before Adam and Eve were made. (Genesis 1:26–28; Psalm 8:3–8; Ephesians 2:10)
9. God's Word provides guidance for all sorts of work that is good, and equips people to do it in a right way. (2 Timothy 3:16–17)
10. Good work is for the glory of God, and God-glorifying work is truly good. (Ephesians 2:10; 2 Timothy 3:16–17)
11. Do all your work as working for the Lord, even when not paid for it. (Colossians 3:22–24)
12. People who use their God-given gifts and abilities in their work will excel and receive recognition from others for their work. (Proverbs 22:29; Matthew 25:14–29)
13. A good reputation is better than riches. (Proverbs 22:1; 28:6)
14. Private property rights are to be protected without bias or favoritism. (Exodus 20:15; 22:1–15; Deuteronomy 19:14; Proverbs 22:28; 31:16–24; 1 Kings 4:25; Ezekiel 46:18; Micah 4:4; Matthew 20:15)
15. People who have legal rights or responsibilities for property will have greater incentive to take care of those things and be more concerned about their loss or abuse. (Luke 15:1–14; John 10:12–13)
16. Those who do the work should partake of the reward. (Proverbs 27:18; 31:31; 1 Timothy 5:18; 2 Timothy 2:6)
17. Contracts are to be fulfilled and evenhandedly enforced, regardless of the financial state of either party. (Exodus 22:9; Leviticus 19:15; Proverbs 29:14; Galatians 3:15; James 2:8–9)
18. Those who squander resources are unwise, and such actions will lead to want. (Proverbs 21:20; Luke 15:13–16)
19. God despises false measures of value, and gains made from deception are an abomination to Him, but He delights in honest valuations. (Leviticus 19:36; Proverbs 11:1; 16:11; 20:10; Amos 8:4–8)

20. Creating added value that generates gain above cost (i.e., producing profit) can benefit both producers and consumers and allow each to bless the other. (Proverbs 13:11; 14:23; 31:10–31)
21. Possessing little money, yet having respect for the Lord, is better than having great riches with disregard for the Lord. (Psalm 37:16; Proverbs 15:16)
22. Laziness leads to poverty, but diligence and discipline keep it at bay. (Proverbs 6:6–11; 10:4; 12:11; 13:4; 24:30–34)
23. With wealth comes the responsibility to use it rightly. (Proverbs 3:9–10; 1 Timothy 6:17–19)
24. God loves a cheerful giver, at work and elsewhere. (2 Corinthians 9:7)
25. God seeks to do His will on earth as it is done in heaven, and by His grace He will work through redeemed people to bring His light to every sphere of life. (Matthew 28:18–20; 5:14–16; Luke 11:2)

Putting academic subjects into the context of the bigger picture of work and human flourishing is not rocket science. Yet it does require some thought on the part of teachers. Let me give you three short examples of putting academic subjects into the context of the bigger picture of work and human flourishing:

1. A third-grade teacher does a unit of study on the local community, including the topic of police service. The teacher asks the following questions to help students connect the dots between the work of the police and the bigger picture:
   » How do you think God looks at police work? Why?
   » How does the work of a policeman relate to the First Commission of Genesis 1:26–28?
   » How can God be glorified through police work? How can He be dishonored?
2. A middle-school science teacher does a unit on the ocean, including the topic of fish. The teacher asks the following questions to help students connect the dots between fish and the bigger picture:
   » How do fish fit into God's purpose for human beings?
   » What responsibilities do humans have with respect to fish?
   » Why do you think God created fish?
3. A high school literature teacher does a unit of study on Shakespeare's *Macbeth*. The teacher asks the following questions to help students connect the dots between this play and the bigger picture:

» What's wrong with human ambition? What's right with human ambition?
» What specific changes in Macbeth's thinking would he have had to make in order for him to glorify God through his work?
» How does the story of Macbeth relate to your current work as a student?

There are many more ways to "contextualize" academic content, but the above examples provide a few samples.

Back to Real Basics

When students solve math problems, they are governing over that part of God's stuff we call "numbers." When they create a piece of art, they're ruling over that part of God's stuff we call "paper," "charcoal," and "watercolor." When they write an essay, they're governing over that part of God's stuff we call "language" and "logic." When they play soccer, they're ruling over that part of God's good stuff we call "legs and feet," not to mention soccer balls and goal posts. When they do science experiments, they're taking dominion over that part of God's good stuff we call "chemicals" and "electricity."

When students put all the things they learn in school into the larger context of God's intention for human beings and His design for the world around us, education takes on remarkable meaning and purpose.

As mentioned earlier, this view of education is not new. Similar views were held by seventeenth-century educators in northern Europe and the British Isles, such as John Comenius and William Ames. Their approach to education laid a foundation for Harvard and Yale in the New World and paved the way for a new nation to flourish, both spiritually and economically.

The challenge today is that our universities no longer train teachers with the same purpose that motivated the early reformers of education. For Comenius and his colleagues, there was no sacred-secular divide. There was no bifurcated compartmentalization of life into "the things of God" and "the things of earth," with a gap between.

Comenius sought to harmonize three "books" he believed were essential for authentic education to take place: (1) the book of God's Word (the "special revelation" of the Bible), (2) the book of God's works (the "general revelation" of creation), and (3) the book of human reason.

There is evidence to support the belief that the three books appearing in the Harvard crest are those three "books" Comenius saw as essential to learning: *human reason submitted to God's Word and His works.*

Below is the original Harvard shield from the seventeenth century:

Surrounding the shield in Latin is the original Harvard motto: *Veritas Christo et Ecclesiae*, "Truth for Christ and the Church." On the shield you will see the top two books (God's Word and God's works) both facing the viewer, while the lower book (human reason) is turned facing the other two. An "arrow" above the lower book points upward toward the higher two books.

Consider these words from *A History of Harvard University, from Its Foundation, in the Year 1636, to the Period of the American Revolution* by Benjamin Peirce, published in 1833. At the end of this chapter, you will find "Rules and Precepts that are observed in the Colledge." Rules #2 and #3 are:

> (2) Let every student be plainly instructed, and earnestly pressed to consider well, the maine end of his life and studies is, *to know God and Jesus Christ which is eternall life*, John. xvii.3. and therefore to lay Christ in the bottome, as the only foundation of all sound knowledge and learning. And seeing the Lord only giveth wisedome, let every one seriously set himselfe by prayer in secret to seeke it of him. Prov. ii.3. (3) Every one shall so exercise himselfe in reading of the Scripture twice a day, that he shall be ready to give such an account of his proficiency therein, both in theoreticall observations of the language, and logick, and in practicall and spiritual truths, as his Tutor shall require, according to his ability; seeing *the entrance of the word*

> *giveth light, it giveth understanding to the simple.* Psalm cxix. 130. (Emphases in the original.)

Below is the Harvard crest as it appears today:

Note that the lower book (human reason) is no longer turned toward the other two. The arrow pointing upward toward the book of God's Word and the book of God's works has been removed, and the Latin motto, *Truth for Christ and the Church*, is gone. Although *Veritas* ("truth") still appears, it certainly is not the same *Veritas* the founders had in mind. The motto replaced by a Greek laurel wreath says it all.

Yale was established in 1701 by a group of pastors who pooled their books to form the first library. The purpose of the new school was that "[y]outh may be instructed in the Arts and Sciences who through the blessing of God may be fitted for Publick employment both in Church and Civil State." No sacred-secular divide here.

I am not suggesting the Puritans got it right in every respect.[36] But I am suggesting that we recover the lost purpose for learning that motivated them. It was a compelling purpose that brought extraordinary meaning to learning and incentive for students like Jonathan Edwards, who graduated from Yale in 1721. He was a theologian, pastor, missionary to Native Americans, and the third president of Princeton University. Among his progeny are scores of pastors and missionaries, 120 college professors, 110 attorneys, 60 authors, 30 judges,

13 college or university presidents, 3 congressmen, and 1 vice-president of the United States.

These kinds of people had a compelling purpose that contributed greatly to the "vision of the order of the whole of things" that once united the states of America, as Allan Bloom pointed out in 1987, but has since disappeared from the public square. I believe that's because we have forgotten the *reason* for Harvard and Yale and have lost the very *purpose* for learning itself.

But it's not just a lost purpose for learning; it's a lost purpose for *living*.

Restoring the lost purpose for learning must be done in a way that is (1) *systemic*, (2) *intentional*, and (3) *repeatable*.

By **systemic,** I mean in a way that embeds a theology of work, economics, and human flourishing into *already existing programs*, from math to science, history to literature, and art to sports, by using an *integral* approach rather than adding another "class" or "subject."

By **intentional,** I mean in a way that incorporates a specific theology of work, economics, and human flourishing premises *into the school's written outcomes, standards, and benchmarks* with as much intentionality as with any other academic objectives.

By **repeatable,** I mean in a way that any Christian teacher may accomplish with a sensible amount of prep time, on a consistent basis, in practical ways that can be passed on to new teachers with a reasonable amount of training.

There are specific ways teachers can accomplish the above goals. Space does not permit me to explain them here, but for those who wish to know more about how this can be done, see this information about the Worklife Restoration and Advancement Project, known as the "WRAP": *bmwplan.blogspot.com/2018/02/creating-and-maintaining-distinctly.html.*

It is time for a course correction. I am hereby calling all elementary and secondary schools that bear the name "Christian" to engage in this challenge through embedding biblical premises of work, economics, and human flourishing into the standard elementary and secondary curriculum from preschool through high school, in brick-and-mortar schools, online schools, home schools, Sunday schools, or underground schools in ways that are systemic, intentional, and repeatable, by God's grace.

Will you join Worldview Matters® in this cause? Please view a four-minute animated video that summarizes much of what I have written here, at *youtu.be/v9ux8UeqYFM.*

As a concerned educator, a grandparent of 12, and a U.S. citizen for seventy years, I am compelled to speak out about the seriousness of our condition as a nation. A few years ago, our national leaders were discussing putting armed guards at schoolhouse doors and having teachers carry concealed weapons. Today, whole cities are talking about defunding their police forces, with one major U.S. school district being pressured by the teachers' union to remove all police presence from their public schools [*latimes.com/california/story/2020-06-08/defund-school-police-utla-blm*]. The "left" and the "right" are at war. At the same time, young people are leaving the church as never before.

Our current trajectory has a painful terminus. If we continue to keep the Lord at a distance, the outcome will be a fallen nation. No doubt about it. There is only one way to "make our nation great again," and that is His way. Remarkably, this is the one way that most of our citizens (and our leaders) will not tolerate.

I created an animated video about all of this, and it is not a happy one. It is rather unpleasant to watch. It contains some difficult words for pastors, for the church, for parents, for state-run schools, and for Christian schools.

A friend, after viewing this video, titled *Not Far Away*, wrote to me: "The impact of the video is to demonize the schools, and the administrators and about 50 percent of the teachers and many of the administrators in those schools who claim to be evangelicals." He was not happy with what I had created. Another friend asked, "How do we help evangelicals who have kids in public schools, or who are public school teachers, or administrators, to 'hear' this message and not feel condemned or helpless, or angry?"

This is a great question!

Certainly, God calls Christians to serve in state-run schools as surely as He chose Joseph to serve in Pharaoh's court and Daniel to serve in Babylon. If you are one of "the chosen," you are not a demon! But are you functioning as a Joseph, a Daniel, or an Esther where God has placed you? These are the kind of Christian teachers and administrators we need in state-run schools today. If you are working inside the public school system, it's past time to speak up.

If you are one such dedicated individual, you may be spending time in a "lions' den," unless you are silent and passive when your time to speak comes up. When it does, remember Esther, who was in the right place "for such a time as this." Your outcome, however, may not be as delightful as was Esther's.

If our churches were training, equipping, and supporting Christian teachers and administrators in *how* to be Daniels and Esthers in state-run schools, that would be one thing. But the churches are not doing this.

It seems to me that if 50 percent of the state school teachers and administrators are evangelical Christians (I doubt this figure), we would have seen a course correction by now. But the hard fact is that it is not possible to reform a system founded on false premises.

Should Christian educators leave the state-run schools? My short answer is, *"Do what the Lord shows you to do."* If God calls you to be in a state-run school, be prepared to do the right thing, as Daniel did. (And be praying as Daniel did, too.) The bigger question, when it comes to educating Christian children, has to do with the churches.

The fact is that most churches are as infected with the SSD as the schools. The majority of young people from Christian homes and churches are thinking more like their secularized textbooks than like the Bible. It only makes sense that a 13-year dose of secularism through secularizing schools would be a major contributor to the secularization of society. How could it not be?

Yes, there are some Daniels and Esthers in our state-run schools. However, Barna tells us that the percentage of those in "Generation Z" (those born in 1999 or later) who identify as atheist is double that of the U.S. adult population, and only 63 percent of America's teens who identify as Christian believe that Jesus is the Son of the one true God. (How does Gen Z define the term "Christian?")

Have we lost the culture war? If we mean "Have we lost the Christian consensus?" the answer is an emphatic *yes.*

A "new normal" is permeating our schools and U.S. culture at large. Some youth are swimming against the tide, yet few are able to withstand the undertow. It's hard enough without attending the secularizing schools. The "Christian consensus" of pre-1960 existed long ago in a galaxy far away. Secularizing schools (both the state-run type and the "Christian" type) has played a significant role in this development.

Here is the bottom line: "The time has come for God's judgment, and it is beginning with the testing of his own people" (1 Peter 4:17, Living Water Translation).

Hope for the future lies with God's own people. But the church cannot bypass the Lord's testing in the process. *We're in it.*

Grace to you, and peace.

Onward and upward.

Theological understanding means nothing if it is not applied. This is true with a theology of education. The theological implication of education that came out of the reformation and was extended by the Puritans to what became the United States of America, was manifested in the homes as home education. This next chapter is written by Scott and Kimberly Allen about their journey as a home education family.

Christian Overman, who wrote Chapter Five, holds a Master of Education degree from Seattle Pacific University, where he studied under Dr. Albert E. Greene Jr., with an emphasis on Philosophy of Christian Education. He holds a Doctor of Ministry degree from Bakke Graduate University, with an emphasis on Theology of Work. He also studied under Chuck Colson in his Centurions Program. Dr. Overman served as principal of a Christian school for 14 years, and he is an adjunct faculty member of Seattle Pacific University. Dr. Overman has been teaching courses on biblical worldview since 1980 for audiences in Europe, Africa, Asia, Central and South America, and North America. He is the founder of Worldview Matters." He and his wife, Kathy (married since 1970), reside near Seattle, Washington. They have four adult children and twelve grandchildren.

Since 2000, Worldview Matters® has been helping followers of Christ recover from secularized thought and make relevant and meaningful connections between the biblical worldview and everyday life. Worldview Matters® assists followers of Christ in living out the implications of biblical faith in the context of the workplace, with a special focus on training elementary and secondary school educators on how to embed biblical worldview truths and theology of work into regular academic course content.

For eight years, Dr. Overman served as the Director of Research and Development for The Biblical Worldview Institute, Puyallup, Washington, and a division of Cascade Christian Schools. This organization is dedicated to helping school teachers connect academic subject matter with the bigger picture of a biblical worldview, making biblical worldview assimilation a part of the everyday school culture.

An international speaker, Dr. Overman has taught on the topic of biblical worldview throughout the United States, as well as in Central America, Europe, Asia, and Africa. He is the author of *Assumptions That Affect Our Lives*, *God's Pleasure at Work*, and *The Difference One Life Can Make* and co-author with Don Johnson of *Making the Connections: How to Put Biblical Worldview Integration into Practice.*

Worldview Matters® 2800 122nd Place NE, Bellevue, WA 98005; Tel: 425-246-5386; Fax: 206-267-9484; *biblicalworldview.com.*

Bibliography

A free e-book edition of this chapter is available at *issuu.com/christianoverman/docs/the_lost_purpose_for_learning.docx*

A hard-copy version is available at *biblicalworldview.com/bookstore.html.*

For a complete course of study on theology of work and human flourishing written for secondary level students, yet suitable for adults of all ages, we recommend the e-text *God's Pleasure at Work & The Difference One Life*

Can Make: An Introduction to Faith, Work and Purpose. See *maximize-meaning.blogspot.com*.

I urge you to view the short, animated video mentioned above, *Not Far Away*: *youtu.be/Igd74KblPvU*.

Allen, Scott D. 2011. *Beyond the Sacred-Secular Divide*. Seattle: YWAM Publishing.

———. 2020. *Why Social Justice Is Not Biblical Justice: An Urgent Appeal to Fellow Christians in a Time of Social Crisis*. Grand Rapids: Credo House Publishing.

Beckett, John. 2006. *Loving Monday*. Downers Grove, IL: IVP.

Crouch, Andy. 2008. *Culture Making*. Downers Grove, IL: IVP.

Eldred, Ken. 2016. *The Integrated Life*. Elevate Faith.

Erisman, Albert M. 2015. *The Accidental Executive: Lessons on Business, Faith, and Calling from the Life of Joseph*. Peabody, MA: Hendrickson Publishers.

Fikkert, Bryan, and Steve Corbett. 2009. *When Helping Hurts*. Chicago: Moody.

Keller, Tim, with Katherine Leary Alsdorf. 2012. *Every Good Endeavor*. New York: Viking Press.

Mangalwadi, Vishal. 2009. *Truth and Transformation*. Seattle: YWAM Publishing.

Miller, Darrow L., with Marit Newton. 2009. *LifeWork*. Seattle: YWAM Publishing.

Nelson, Tom. 2011. *Work Matters*. Wheaton, IL: Crossway.

Overman, Christian. 2007. *Assumptions That Affect Our Lives*. Bellevue, WA: Ablaze Publishing.

Overman, Christian, with Chris Hare. 2016. *God's Pleasure at Work & The Difference One Life Can Make: An Introduction to Faith, Work and Purpose*. Pennsauken, NJ: BookBaby.

Peabody, Larry. 2010. *Job-Shadowing Daniel*. Parker, CO: Outskirts Press.

Pearcey, Nancy. 2004. *Total Truth*. Wheaton, IL: Crossway.

Schultz, Glen. 1998. *Kingdom Education*. Nashville: Lifeway.

Self, Charlie. 2012. *Flourishing Churches & Communities*. Grand Rapids: Christian's Library Press.

Sherman, Amy L. 2011. *Kingdom Calling*. Downers Grove, IL: IVP.

Sherman, Doug, and William Hendricks. 1987. *Your Work Matters to God*. Colorado Springs, CO: NavPress.

Stevens, R. Paul. 2010. *The Other Six Days: Vocation, Work, and Ministry in Biblical Perspective*. Grand Rapids: Eerdmans.

Strandness, Erik. 2014. *The Director's Cut*. Bloomington, IN: Westbow Press.

Theology of Work Project. 2015. *Theology of Work Bible Commentary* (5 Volumes). Peabody, MA: Hendrickson Publishers.

Veith, Gene Edward Jr. 2002. *God at Work*. Wheaton, IL: Crossway.

Ward, Mark L. Jr., ed. 2015. *Biblical Worldview: Creation, Fall, Redemption*. Greenville, SC: BJU Press.

Whelchel, Hugh. 2012. *How Then Should We Work*. Bloomington, IN: Westbow Press.

Wolters, Albert. 1985. *Creation Regained*. Grand Rapids: Eerdmans.

SIX

Prayerfully Consider Home Education

Scott and Kimberly Allen

On a beautiful, warm Southern California evening, we were out for a walk with a friend from college, Don McLean, and his wife, Christine. They had both joined the international relief and development organization Food for the Hungry after university and had lived for two years in Bolivia. We had likewise joined Food for the Hungry, serving for two years in Japan. Now both couples were back in the U.S. with young children and growing families. SG-6

Don and Christine had recently chosen to home educate, which was a foreign concept to me. When I (Scott) was growing up in small-town Oregon in the 1970s, nobody homeschooled their children. Like everyone else, I attended public schools from kindergarten through high school. It was all I knew. Home educating sounded exotic, even extreme.

As we chatted, I asked Don why he and Christine had come to this decision. I joked, asking if they had joined some fringe fundamentalist church.

Don paused, responding to my question with a question of his own. This turned out to be a major turning point in my life, and in the life of my wife and children. In fact, the ripples of that simple question may influence generations:

"Who has the primary responsibility for educating your children, Scott?"

I don't recall what my reaction was, but likely my first thought would have been something along the lines of "the state" or "the public schools." But almost immediately, I knew that these answers were not right. I answered, "I suppose Kim and I do."

Don smiled. He knew, as I did, that the Bible is crystal clear on this question.

> These words that I command you today shall be on your heart. You shall teach them diligently to your children, and shall talk of them when you sit in your house, and when you walk by the way, and when you lie down, and when you rise. (Deuteronomy 6:6–7)

> Train up a child in the way he should go;
> even when he is old he will not depart from it. (Proverbs 22:6)

> Fathers, do not provoke your children to anger, but *bring them up in the discipline and instruction of the Lord.* (Ephesians 6:4, emphasis added).

The next day, I talked with Kimberly. As is typical, she was already ahead of me. She had been sensing a call to home educate our kids as well and was excited to try. But suddenly my practical side kicked in. Could we *afford* to home educate our kids? There would be the costs for a curriculum, but more than that, the lost income from Kimberly not being formally employed. We were barely making ends meet on my limited income as a staff person at a Christian ministry. The numbers didn't add up. But Kimberly was ready to take the step of faith before I was. She encouraged me to trust that if God was calling us onto this journey, He would provide, . . . and she was right.

The decision we made that warm night in Southern California with the help of our dear friends turned out to be one of the best we've ever made.

Lessons Learned

As we look back over the twenty-plus years that we've been home educating our five children, three of whom have now graduated from university, here are some of the biggest lessons we've learned along the way.

Education as a way of life

Home educating taught us the difference between schooling and education. Schooling is an activity; education is a way of life—a lifelong endeavor. At first, we set time aside during the day to formally "school" the kids. Eventually, however, our schooling time bled over into the rest of the day, and into our whole lives. Our family began to love learning in a new way.

We would begin the day with Bible reading, discussion, and prayer. Meals became important times for learning and discussion. In the evenings, Kim started handing me books to read to the kids, and this grew into a passion for me, and a favorite activity for all the kids. When we finally got to Tolkien's Lord of the Rings trilogy, I wanted to keep reading it over and over. The discussions that our reading times engendered were precious to all of us. We quickly discovered that every part of life provided incredible opportunities for learning.

Kimberly and I had discovered a new way to think about school and education, and really, what it means to be a family. In many respects, home education is far more than "education." For us, it was about rediscovering what the Bible teaches us about being as families. Now, grandparents, aunts, uncles, friends, and church members aren't simply family members or friends—they are potential educators of our children who can offer incredible life experiences and wisdom.

Education had become a joyful way of life, adding incredible purpose and meaning into our home.

A God-centered, God-saturated education

Home education allows you to place God at the very center and foundation of education, exactly where He belongs. "For by him all things were created, in heaven and on earth, visible and invisible, whether thrones or dominions or rulers or authorities—all things were created through him and for him" (Colossians 1:16). Because this is true, nothing can be rightly understood apart from God.

Public schools typically enforce a strict separation between "religion" and education. Religious beliefs are deemed personal, not public. You are free to worship whatever god you choose in the privacy of your home, church, synagogue, temple, or mosque, but not in the classroom or public square. In practice, subjects such as algebra, literature, biology, and history are taught in a strictly secular way. The God of Genesis 1:1 doesn't factor in at all.

After twelve years of this kind of public education, most Christian youth are firmly inculcated with a deistic, sacred-secular mindset. God is relegated to the personal, private, and "spiritual" part of our lives. After all, for twelve years He apparently had nothing to do with academic subjects, and very little to do with life beyond church and private devotions. This is a form of indoctrination that has only worsened since my days in Oregon's public schools.

In fact, today public education actively inculcates not a strictly secular worldview as in my student days but a quasi-religious ideology known in academic circles as critical social theory, mixing postmodern and neo-Marxist presuppositions. In effect, public schools have abandoned the pretense of religious neutrality and are pushing an atheistic religion. This new faith is distinct and incompatible with biblical Christianity in its view of ultimate reality, power, authority, human nature, morality (particularly as it relates to marriage, family, and sexuality), epistemology, and much more.[1]

By contrast, home educators are free to place the true and living God at the center of everything, where He belongs. This freedom disciplined Kimberly and me to think in fresh ways about academic subjects. We fleshed out a biblical worldview that began with biblical answers to the most fundamental questions: What is ultimately real? What is true? What is good? Who are we? How should we relate to others and creation? Why does evil exist? How do we respond to it? What happens after we die? In short, we were being trained to think biblically about *everything*. Not only did this affect our children during their homeschooled years but also into their university and postgrad years. The biblical worldview had been so deeply engrained in them that when the loud voice of the world came ringing through their ears later on in life, they had a solid foundation to fall back on. For someone shaped by a supposed sacred-secular divide, this new approach to knowledge was life-changing.

Evangelization and discipleship

Home education presented us with a very natural way to evangelize and disciple our children. When we place God at the center of life and education, we gain a wonderful opportunity to display what a living and active faith looks like to our children, who may thus be more likely to fall in love with Jesus and commit their lives to His service.

When our children see us attempting to live out our faith day in and day out—often making mistakes, often failing, but asking for mercy and forgiveness and leaning on God's mercy, which is new every morning—they begin to know God in a real and personal way.

Helpfully, home education also blurs the line between education and discipleship. It enables us to link education, discipleship, and training in virtuous self-government and character formation into a seamless whole. Education encompasses all of life and provides endless opportunities to form and shape our children into passionate disciples. God calls His church to share the gospel with nonbelievers and disciple them toward Christ-likeness, with the goal of influencing and blessing entire nations. The home is where this process must start. How can we evangelize and disciple our nations if we bypass the most basic society we influence? The reformation of the church, and revival in our nations, should begin in our families. This was always God's design. We've just lost sight of it.

Home education allows space for children to become self-motivated learners

Public education follows what some call a "factory model." Because it deals with large numbers of kids, it is forced to treat them more or less the same as they work through the system. There is little time for our children to explore areas of particular interest or discover their unique interests and gifts.

Home education, by contrast, allows children to dive deeply into particular areas of interest. This flexibility allows them to develop their natural, God-given love for learning and, over time, develop the skills to become self-motivated learners.

At the same time, because they are not dealing with thirty children at one time, parents are able to discover their children's interests, giftings, and challenges more deeply, and guide them and help them grow in these areas.

Our oldest son struggles with dyslexia. When Kimberly and I became aware of this, we did a deep dive into the nature of this condition and the best ways to help our son. We learned that while dyslexia makes it very difficult (or in some cases, nearly impossible) to learn to read using a traditional phonics-based approach, those with it tend to be highly creative with uncanny abilities to see things in a different light. With this knowledge, we helped our son improve his reading with dyslexic-specific approaches. We also encouraged him to use his strong gifts of creativity and outside-the-box thinking. We began to see dyslexia not as a disability but a powerful *other*-ability—a God-given one. Home education enabled us to give focused attention to our son. This is simply not possible in a factory approach.

Flexibility and simplicity

Home education in many ways, simplified our life. We were free to set the agenda and the schedule for our children. If we wanted to take a "field trip" to a local fire station, museum, or business, or do a service project on a particular day, we didn't have to negotiate with the educational system, teachers, and administrators for their approval. There were no endless fundraising campaigns for extracurricular activities. We didn't have to constantly review curricula for false and objectionable material, and then negotiate with the educational bureaucrats to excuse our kids from being exposed to it.

Home education has also allowed us to determine the right *time* for our children to be exposed to ideas such as Darwinism, postmodernism, secularism, and secular views on sexuality, race, gender, and the broader social justice ideology. Home education allowed us to nurture them deeply during their elementary school years in what is good, true, and beautiful, while protecting their innocence. But as they matured in faith in their middle school years, we introduced these difficult topics by comparing and contrasting them with biblical teaching.

In public schools, by contrast, teachers and peers determine when our kids learn about these things. Unfortunately, the time of introduction is getting earlier and earlier. Our kids in public schools are being discipled into false, unbiblical ideas at a very young age, and parents struggle to overcome all this in the few hours they have at home or in the church.

As we grew in our roles as home educators, Kimberly and I quickly began to see fruit in our children's lives. As we nurtured their innate hunger to learn and to know the true, living God, by His grace their faith grew deep, sincere, and vibrant.

Typical Barriers

Here are a few common barriers people who are considering home education face, along with encouragement on how to surmount them.

I don't get along with my kids

This barrier is perhaps the one we hear most often. "I could never home school my kids." "We are so different; we just end up getting on each other's nerves."

It is a real challenge. We understand. Like everyone else, our kids are fallen people with built-in inclinations toward selfishness and self-centeredness. They can be lazy, touchy, grouchy, irritating, and sometimes impossible. (So can we, by the way.)

But the idea that I don't get along with my kids and therefore will send them to public school may be an avoidance strategy about something that God wants us to confront.

Let's face it. It is always hardest to practice our Christian faith with those who know us intimately. We can't hide our faults or hang-ups. Yet God wants us in these very relationships to practice obedience, to love one another, to forgive one another, to confess our sins and shortcomings, to have mercy with one another. Parents should take the lead in these areas. When conflict or tension arises, we should practice biblical teaching on reconciliation, confess our failures, short tempers, angry outbursts, and more. We should ask God for strength to grow in these weak areas. Such an example of humility and transparency becomes a powerful lesson for our children. They learn by our imperfect but growing example what living the Christian life is all about.

Instead of seeing conflict with kids as a barrier, why not see it as an opportunity for everyone to put faith into practice and live it out in the most basic relationships? Simple steps of obedience to biblical commands to love, confess, confront, and forgive pay lifetime dividends. If these practices can be learned in the family, they can be practiced in relationships beyond the home.

Peer pressure from family and friends

Although the numbers of people who are home educating is growing rapidly, it is still a relatively small community. So often those we are closest to—our family members, friends, and sometimes even the leaders of our churches—will not understand. Many will challenge us about our choice. Some will likely disapprove.

One way to respond is simply to say that you are trying home education for a year at a time. If it turns out not to work, you can always change. Most people will understand this and recognize your freedom to give it a try. Then, if you choose to continue, as each year goes by, and your children and family exhibit the benefits of home education, these folks will be less likely to criticize your choice.

Socialization

A very common barrier is the question, "How will my children become properly socialized if they are not with their peers in school?" It reflects the misconception that home education is "lone" education. We do not favor any approach to education that is done alone, or in isolation, with a child alone in a room with a computer.

Home education, ideally, will be done in community, together with siblings, extended family members, and other home school families. Parents will work in networks or co-ops so they can share teaching responsibilities based on their particular skills or expertise. As home education has grown, the opportunities to connect and work with other home school families has grown as well. In many areas the home education community is vibrant, and novice home educators have the opportunity to build cooperative relationships with other home educators in their areas. Regardless, you should find other people who support you, such as grandparents, uncles, or aunts.

The idea that home-educated children are not socialized is simply false. They *are* socialized, but in a different way than their public-school peers. Their group may include not only other children or youth, but newborn babies, young adults, and seniors. They are frequently accustomed to relating with a wide variety of people, including those from different cultural backgrounds. Yes, home-educated children are indeed socialized!

But let us remember that *how* your children are socialized is critical. Their closest friends and mentors *should* be the ones who reinforce their biblical beliefs and values rather than the ones who draw them away from them. Home education provides an environment to make this possible. As the Bible says, "By wisdom a house is built, and by understanding it is established" (Proverbs 24:3).

We can't afford it

This was one of my first reactions to the idea of home education. There is a real cost, and it may seem difficult, if not impossible, to see how the numbers will add up. The main cost is the loss of income from the spouse who is the primary home educator.

We strongly urge newly married couples to build the family budget around the salary of just one breadwinner so that his or her spouse may be devoted to home education full time. This may seem impossible, but simplifying your lifestyle, choosing a less expensive home or car, or foregoing things such as gym memberships or cable television should all be considered. These material costs are real, but in comparison with what you will gain in your home life and the quality of education and character development in your children over the long term, this trade-off is a no-brainer.

Even if you can't see a way to take the step of home education financially, I encourage you to prayerfully take a step of faith and ask God to provide. You may discover that, as in our case, He answers that prayer. For us, the Lord's provision came in unanticipated and faith-building ways, often daily and yearly, like manna from heaven. If God has called you, He will provide.

I'm not a trained expert on education

Many people think, "Who am I to think I could do a better job educating my child than someone who has a degree in education? I should leave this job to the experts." Our teachers deserve our respect and appreciation for their skill and hard work, but the idea that you don't have the ability to teach your own children is false. In many respects, you are far *better* equipped to teach them. You know them intimately. You know their strengths and weaknesses. You can tailor their education accordingly, helping them to grow in areas where they show great potential.

As the children grow into their junior and senior high years, you can rely on outstanding home education curricular alternatives, particularly in mathematics, science, writing, and grammar, often with video tutorials. Co-ops are also incredibly helpful. Lean on other parents who have particular strengths or backgrounds in the humanities, sciences, mathematics, and so on. Teach to your strengths and allow others to share their strengths and knowledge. You'll be surprised at just how many knowledgeable people are in your social circles once you start looking for them.

You don't have to be an expert on any given subject. You just need to be one step ahead of your kids. As you go through the curriculum with them, you will need to read and study in advance, refreshing your own teaching in these areas. In the process, *you* will become more educated, more able to quickly appreciate the joy and excitement of learning as you prepare to teach your children what you've learned.

Prayerfully Consider Home Education

Home education isn't easy, but we've seen it bear wonderful fruit in our children and family. It has forged deep bonds between us and our children, and among the children. In our home education journey—for that is what it is, a journey—each of us has grown deeper in our faith and knowledge of biblical truth as it applies to all areas of life.

Certainly, home education isn't for everyone. Other excellent choices exist, including private Christian schools or even excellent public or charter schools. But as you consider educational options for your children, please prayerfully and carefully consider home education. Don't let the barriers scare you off. Take a step of faith and obedience and see how God blesses that decision and opens up ways you didn't think were possible.

While we are advocates for home education, we understand and respect that not everyone is. We simply want to encourage you to seek the Lord, develop your own convictions and live by them, and don't judge the convictions of others.

Romans 14:1–22 provides helpful instruction in this area. Some key paraphrased takeaways:

> Don't quarrel over disputable matters. Who are you to judge someone else's servant? To their own master, servants stand or fall. And they will stand, for the Lord is able to make them stand.
>
> Let us stop passing judgment on one another. Instead, make up your mind not to put any stumbling block or obstacle in the way of a brother or sister.
>
> Make every effort to do what leads to peace and to mutual edification.
>
> So, whatever you believe about these things, keep it between yourself and God.

But let's remember that as the family goes, so goes the nation. Perhaps the greatest thing any of us can do for the discipleship of our communities and nations is to raise our children in a way that places God at the very center and imparts to them deep faith, biblical virtues, and the capacity to self-govern.

Jonathan Edwards (1703–1758) stands among the finest theologians, pastors, and intellectuals the United States has ever produced. He played a central role in the First Great Awakening, authored many books, preached countless sermons, and inspired generations of missionaries. Yet his greatest legacy is one he shares with his wife, Sarah—the amazing influence their godly offspring had on the United States across many generations. Jonathan and Sarah Edwards are prime examples of how God can use the uniquely multigenerational institution of the family to bless an entire nation. In the span of 150 years, from this one couple came:

- Thirteen college presidents and sixty-five college professors
- One hundred lawyers and thirty judges
- Sixty-six medical doctors
- Three United States Senators, three governors of states, three mayors of large cities, and a Vice President of the United States.
- Leaders in banking, commerce, and industry
- Over one hundred cross-cultural missionaries.[2]

This kind of culture-shaping influence did not happen by accident. It is the fruit of a marriage built upon the teachings of the Bible. Could your family have a similar impact on your nation? A husband and wife who adopt this vision see in their children their most important mission in life.

"Children are a heritage from the Lord . . . like arrows in the hand of a warrior" (Psalm 127:3, 4). Arrows are weapons of war. Our children are likened to arrows in a battle against an enemy. The battle is for the advancement of God's kingdom and the discipling of nations. Our enemy is Satan.

Why arrows?

With a sword, a soldier can attack only as far as he can reach. But a properly made arrow can strike an enemy far beyond. Likewise, our children should far surpass us in their godly maturity and impact for Christ's kingdom. And their children should advance even further.

Allow this to be your vision for educating your children—a vision to raise up a generation of warrior-servants who will advance boldly against the enemy in every sphere of society.

Theological understanding means nothing if it is not applied. This is true with a theology of governance, science, public health, education, etc. While Martin Luther wanted to reform the Church, John Calvin understood that the Church's job was not simply to teach sound biblical principles but to apply theological understanding to all areas of life. The next chapter is a case study of how the biblical world and life view, as manifest through Calvin's teaching of the whole council of God, changed Geneva and eventually Northern Europe and laid the foundation for the American experiment.

Scott and Kimberly Allen, home education parents, have written Chapter Six of this book. Scott has spent his entire career in the area of Christian community development, poverty alleviation, and justice ministry. His passion is to help Christians understand the biblical worldview as the only sure foundation for healthy, flourishing lives, communities, and cultures.

He is cofounder and president of the Disciple Nations Alliance (*www.disciplenations.org*), an international discipleship ministry that exists "to equip the Church to rise to her full potential as God's principal agent in restoring, healing, and blessing broken nations." The DNA is active in more than 100 countries worldwide.

After serving with the international development organization Food for the Hungry International for 19 years in both the United States and Japan, Scott teamed up with his friends and mentors, Darrow Miller and Bob Moffitt, to launch the Disciple Nations Alliance in 2008.

Scott is author and co-author of several books, including *Why Social Justice Is Not Biblical Justice: An Urgent Appeal to Fellow Christians in a Time of Social Crisis* (Credo House Publishers, 2020).

Kimberly is wife to Scott and a proud home school mother of five children. She earned her undergraduate degree in international relations from Willamette University in Salem, Oregon, and served for three years as a missionary in Osaka, Japan, before marrying Scott in 1992.

Disciple Nations Alliance, Secretariat Office, 1110 E. Missouri Ave., #393, Phoenix, Arizona 85014; Tel.: 602-386-4560; Fax: 602-386-4564; info@disciplenations.org; *disciplenations.org*.

SEVEN

John Calvin in Geneva: A Nation-Building Missionary

Thomas A. Bloomer

Geneva, nestled at the foot of the Alps at the crossroads of several major traveling routes, has been a center of influence since before the Roman Empire, trading both goods and ideas throughout Europe. Today, this small city is actually the diplomatic capital of the world, as 70 percent of the work of the United Nations is done there, and powerful organizations such as the World Trade Organization have their headquarters there. Its story is a rich tapestry of all the elements of a blockbuster movie: violence, corruption, intrigue, and courage in the face of great risk and injustice. In Geneva we can learn important lessons on the process of discipling a nation, as well as vital warnings of what happens when the church fails in its mandate. 

During the Middle Ages, Geneva was a wild town. The streets teemed with crowds, as people from all over Europe passed through on their way to France, Italy, Germany, or Austria. With more inns per capita than any other city of its time, the city was full of partying traders, petty criminals, political refugees, spies, and sailors from Lake Geneva. Drunkenness was common, and the houses of prostitution did a good business. The city trade fairs were particularly famous; during those events the town was wide open and filled with people.

However, as the sixteenth century began, competition from France markedly reduced attendance at the fairs, and the walls of the city fell into disrepair. People were poor, families were falling apart, and the future looked grim. Geneva was called the smelliest city of Europe.

Much of the responsibility lay with the Roman Church. All over Europe people were turning away, disgusted by the corruption and hypocrisy. The church was literally selling salvation, as people had to pay large amounts of cash to be sure of escaping hell. In Geneva, the priests were not only immoral themselves but were also running houses of prostitution. In losing its purity, the church lost its power, and so squandered its authority and its leadership. The people actually ran the Bishop of Geneva out of town in 1530, and most of the city's nobles left with him. The spiritual and moral vacuum soon had major political and economic consequences. Geneva was in crisis.

Europeans were grappling with life and death questions: "How can we live? Is there a better way to take care of our families? Run the economy? Take care of the poor? What about school for the children? How should we defend ourselves? What responsibility does each citizen have?" As in many countries of the world today, solutions were needed for government, the economy, defense, schools, family life, and morality. The people were asking, and the church had no answers.

As the church became increasingly corrupt and burdensome on people's lives, there were stirrings across Europe for a more biblical Christianity. The underlying beliefs of this Reformation movement were that the Bible must be the source of authority to shape every aspect of people's lives, and the foundation of truth for entire communities and nations. One vital step toward this goal was for the people to have the Word of God in their language and their homes. Sadly, but not surprisingly, resistance to this came from the Catholic Church itself, which in turn incited the government to persecute these believers. Forced to flee their homes, the Protestants spread the movement around Europe as they relocated.

William Farel, the redheaded, hot-tempered French evangelist, came into the vacuum that was Geneva in 1531. His strategy was simple but very effective: Go into a city, do some outrageous things, get everybody all stirred up, and then get run out of town. His overall goal: Make sure that everyone was angry enough to be talking about this new religion of the Protestant Reformers.

Once, he stopped to go into a church service and got so upset about what the priest was preaching that he went up to the front, pushed the priest out of the pulpit, and began preaching himself. Another time he saw priests leading a procession with relics down by the side of the river, and he ran over and pushed both priests and relics into the water. He was literally run out of Geneva by the monks of the cathedral.

Farel always managed to get out just in time. A good sense of timing is crucial for that kind of ministry strategy!

After he was kicked out of Geneva, one of Farel's co-workers, the Frenchman Antoine Froment, started a school to teach children to read by using the Bible. Many adults wanted to learn how to read as well, so they also came to his school. Froment got so excited one day in 1534 that he came to the market square and jumped up on one of the market tables and started preaching. Some of the authorities came to listen, and at one point Froment got carried away and cried out, "We must reform the church in order to reform the nation!" That offended the authorities so much that they arrested him and then kicked him out of town.

When the Bishop had been run out of Geneva, so many of the church and political leaders left that there was a leadership vacuum in the city. Businessmen whose salvation was rooted in the Reformation had migrated to the city; they began small groups to meet for study and prayer. The simplicity and disciplined lifestyles of the Protestant Reformers stood in stark contrast to the corruption of the church and nobility. City leadership fell to these new leaders; finally, on August 26, 1535, the electors of the city of Geneva voted unanimously to become a Reformed Protestant city. They also agreed to the condition that they teach every child in the city to read. One implication of their decision was that the city came under the protection of the Lords of Bern, strong Protestants who continued to mentor the city leaders.

Once the decision was made, the Reformers proceeded to destroy all of the stained-glass windows and statues of the cathedral. They felt that the people had worshipped these images, and therefore the images were considered idolatrous and in need of being destroyed.

However, in contrast to the Lutheran Reformation, they did not believe that all the citizens automatically became Christians just because the electors had voted for the city to be Protestant. The French Reformers believed that every adult had to make a personal commitment to Christ to be saved. To ensure that every person had a chance to respond to Christ, there was a sustained, ongoing effort for many years to proclaim the gospel, even in the streets and marketplaces.

While the electors had been unanimous in their decision that Geneva become a Protestant city, intense debate went on among the population. Many resisted Calvin, others resented the refugees he brought with him, and some were still pro-Catholic. It's hard to appreciate just how big a decision this was for the city. As Catholics, the people were risking excommunication and eternal damnation if this new religion were leading them away from God and His truth.

When the Reformation was finally accepted, it was evident that a pastor-teacher was the crucial need of the city. Farel knew that he was an apostolic evangelist, but not the builder who was so necessary for the reconstruction of the nation. When he heard that John Calvin was in town, Farel immediately went to visit him.

Calvin and Farel had both been students in the theological faculty of the University of Paris when the Reformation started to break out there. They had both been Augustinian monks, and like many others who were reading the New Testament and deciding that the present Roman church was not at all biblical in its practices, they had to flee France for their lives.

After Calvin left, he was shocked to learn that the authorities were proclaiming that the Protestants not only did not have the truth but were just rebels against the church who had no coherent beliefs. Since no defense of the Protestant faith existed in writing in French Europe, this version of events was gaining acceptance. Calvin set out to clearly state what Protestants believed, and the result was the *Institutes of the Christian Religion*. He wrote it for the memory of his friends, as an apologetic in a time of intense conflict, and so that many others would turn to the Bible and to a living faith in Christ. To think of Calvin as an ivory-tower theologian is to seriously underestimate him.

In 1536, at age 27, Calvin was traveling through Geneva, and Farel found him in an inn down by the lake. Farel spoke to him about the situation in the city and called Calvin to join him in rebuilding the nation. Calvin had weak health, and his only ambition at that time was to continue his studies. So, he said to Farel, "No, I can't do that. I need rest and I need to study." Farel got very angry, pointed his long, bony evangelist's finger at Calvin, and thundered, "May God curse you and your studies if you do not join me here in the work He has called you to!" This threatened curse made such an impression on Calvin that he remembered it until the end of his life. He consented to stay and committed his life to the work of God in Geneva.

Calvin cannot be blamed for hesitating to accept Farel's challenge. Geneva was a very difficult place to minister for many reasons. The city authorities, influenced by the Lutheran Protestants, believed that the church should be ruled by the government, including defining who was a Christian, could take communion, or be a priest. In contrast, the leaders of the French Reformation believed that there are different spheres within society, each with its own domain of decision making. They taught that the government held the right to provide for the people's defense and levy taxes for the common needs of society, and the church was subject to its authority only in clearly defined areas.

For twenty years after voting to become a Protestant city, the authorities wanted decision-making power over the church. Calvin had to argue with them for all those years in order to establish the principle that the church should run its own affairs. He also wanted to establish the principle that the church had a primary *teaching* role in society and was to hold individuals and institutions, including the government, accountable to biblical morality. Calvin wasn't always right in the way he saw things, but his noble attempt to rebuild the city on biblical foundations was history-making, the first such attempt outside of Israel.

These differences between the two strains of Reformation theology quickly came into direct conflict. Two years after he came to the city, the city authorities requested that Calvin give communion to the entire population. As French Reformation theologians, Calvin and Farel refused, reasoning that since some of the citizens were living in open sin they could not give communion to people who didn't even pretend to be Christians. The authorities insisted that they serve communion to everyone on Easter Sunday in 1538.

Calvin went to preach in the cathedral that day, and Farel preached in the second parish of the city. They both taught on sin and judgment and proceeded to publicly excommunicate the entire population of Geneva. Then they left town, knowing their ministry was over in the city. Farel went back home to Neuchatel, and Calvin went to Strasbourg to continue his studies.

The authorities at first said "Good riddance," but three years later, at a point of desperation, they came to visit Calvin and his new wife in Strasbourg. They explained that the city was threatened with invasion, which would have meant a return to Catholicism, losing everything they'd worked for. They knew that Calvin had a stronger, clearer vision for rebuilding the city than the rest of the city leaders, and he alone had the personal influence to rally the people to fight and withstand an invasion. The authorities asked him to return and help save the city.

Calvin knew that the cost would be great, but he agreed and went back to Geneva. Changing a nation requires a lifetime commitment, and he gave the rest of his life so that Geneva would be as biblically based a city as possible.

As the word went out that John Calvin had been named the head pastor of Geneva, Protestants all over Europe were electrified. He was well known because of the *Institutes*, and people knew that his ministry in Geneva could be a historic opportunity. In many countries the Protestants had been put to death, or exiled and robbed of their lands and possessions. In others, such as England and some of the Swiss cantons, the Reformation seemed to be gaining a foothold. In Geneva, however, the deeply entrenched social order of church and nobility had been torn down, so in that vacuum there was a unique opportunity for the Reformers to rebuild a city on biblical foundations.

Geneva quickly became a city of refuge for the Protestants. Its streets were filled with Italians, Englishmen, and especially the French. The population of the city, which was only 5,000 before the Reformation, quickly doubled to 10,000. People called it the Protestant Rome and "the city set on a hill." All the Protestants of Europe looked toward Geneva to see what would be built. This small city-state was the laboratory, the pilot project, for the vision of a nation built on biblical principles and living in peace, prosperity, and righteousness.

Even though the city was small, its influence went far and wide. Two young men came to visit Geneva from Holland, were soundly converted, and went back to transmit this new message to William of Orange. Their visit is the reason Holland became Protestant, as he converted to the new faith.

Another example is found in Scotland. When Mary, Queen of Scots, began her persecutions, the number of Protestant refugees coming from Scotland increased dramatically. In 1556 the former prayer chapel of the Bishop was reconsecrated as the church for the English-speaking refugees. John Knox, who was also a refugee, was pastor of the congregation and preached in that church for three years. He studied what Calvin was doing in the city and took it back to Scotland; the influence of Geneva then went to Puritan England and from there to North America.

The strategy of the Reformers was based on three principles:

1. Preaching the gospel to individuals, so that people would be saved and start to be transformed and the church would be restored to biblical purity;
2. Teaching the city, so that people would know how to live, the authorities would know how to govern, and all would know how to work in their different spheres; and
3. Accountability for individuals and the leadership in spheres of society, so that the teaching would not just be theoretical but applied in all areas of life.

The basis of rebuilding the nation was individual conversion, so that the population would put its trust in God. The immediate second step was a systematic, daily, long-term strategy of teaching. The challenge was to build a nation on biblical principles, so Calvin and his team searched the Scriptures and did their best to apply them to the crisis situations in the city. They taught in the churches, but they also pursued city leaders to bring biblical truths into society. Calvin had a legal background, so he approached the needs of the city as a lawyer and not just as a pastor. He had the gifts and training to see the issues wholistically and understand the biblical principles needed to build society, such as defining the structure of the government and the role of the church. He taught across a wide range of issues; examining several areas in some detail illustrates the depth and breadth of his thinking and the impact his teaching had on the nation.

One example of applying the principles of the Word occurred when the walls of the city were literally down. The Reformers called on all the populace to come and rebuild them. Calvin told the citizens that, while they must trust in God, they were also responsible to do everything they could to protect themselves. They could no longer hide behind a nobleman or the church to protect them; they needed to rebuild the walls, arm themselves, and resist the oppressors who were threatening to invade. The pastors were there, too, joining in the stone-by-stone reconstruction of the walls. Calvin taught the people to be responsible and work hard to defend themselves, but he also insisted that only God could protect Geneva, and he exhorted the people to put their trust in the Lord for protection.

This teaching resonated well in the city; the people knew that Switzerland had come into being by citizens uniting and arming themselves against imperial armies. Calvin taught that this approach was profoundly biblical; in fact, until very recently in the country's history, every Swiss male has been required to serve in the citizen army and keep an automatic rifle and ammunition at home. While the Swiss maintain political neutrality in the conflicts among other nations, they have always been ready to defend themselves as a nation. It's interesting to note that Switzerland is the only nation where every man legally possesses a loaded weapon; no other nation in history has trusted its citizens like this.

Another of Calvin's principal ministry concerns was the family. Many of the men of Geneva were irresponsible, prone to drunkenness, and dishonest. The disorder in their lives was one of the causes of the poverty and immorality of the city. So, the Reformers began teaching about individual responsibility, which meant first of all caring for one's family. Each head of household was expected to work hard, pay his bills, give his tithe, and save his money.

But this was not just a teaching about how to achieve and maintain prosperity. Calvin taught that one's work is one's worship. We tend to believe today that work is what you do until Sunday, when you go to worship. But Calvin taught that every believer, not just "full-time workers," has a holy vocation. For example, if you are a shoemaker, that is your vocation. So, you have to work as unto the Lord, since you are presenting that work to Him as worship. Clearly, if your work is your worship, then it has to be done with the utmost integrity and excellence. In fact, when Max Weber, the great German economist, was looking for the sources of the prosperity of the West one hundred years ago, he pointed to Calvin's Geneva.

Another of the sources of Geneva's prosperity was Calvin's teaching concerning financial principles. He told the bankers that they couldn't charge high interest rates, as that constituted the sin of usury as presented in the Bible. He fixed the interest rates at four percent, so that the bankers could have a fair return on their money but people could still afford to borrow and invest. The four-percent interest rate lasted for four centuries in Switzerland, and this practice was one of the long-term sources of Switzerland's prosperity.

One of the most amazing things that happened in Geneva was in education. The citizens had committed to educate their children as part of their decision to become a Protestant city. This commitment was the result of the theological conviction that each person is created in the image of God, each can be in relationship with God directly, and people need only to read the Bible to know how that is supposed to work. A real first in the history of the world was that all the children of a nation, including the girls, were taught to read. Sadly, the people who teach education today have forgotten that literacy for all is a biblical idea.

Calvin also taught about caring for the poor. An organization was established that cared for newly arrived Protestant refugees, widows, and orphans. Anyone who *could* work *had* to work; the poor were considered accountable, too (a principle forgotten in too many countries today). It is said that all Protestant charities have their source in Calvin's organizations in Geneva, since they were copied and adopted throughout the Protestant countries.

In an attempt to bring accountability to deal with the crisis in the family, the Reformers established a kind of citizen tribunal, organized by neighborhood. Any man who beat his wife, or any mother who neglected her children, would be brought before a jury of neighbors and called to account.

Today the excesses of these tribunals are better known than the good they did, and it is true that they provided an easy way for mean-spirited people to settle accounts with neighbors they disliked. But Geneva was in crisis, and people did not know how to care for families, work, and live morally. Invasion threatened, and Calvin knew that if the city were to survive he had only a narrow window of opportunity to teach the populace to become a united, disciplined citizenry able to care for and defend itself.

Accountability was woven into the government structures, as well. The Reformers were convinced of the sinfulness of humankind, especially since the people had had personal experience of the corrupting power of undifferentiated authority. The King of France, as an absolute monarch, could and did decide to put Protestants to death. They knew that any leader or structure that cannot be held accountable will slide inevitably into sin, so they invented a system of government we now call federalism, where power is divided among the executive, legislative, and judicial branches of the government. The judiciary is especially important and must be free and independent.

A further division of powers takes place between the national, or federal, government and the cantons (or states) that make up the nation, and the towns. The Swiss system of federalism provided the model for the Americans who designed their government in the late eighteenth century, since they also mistrusted an all-powerful central government because of their experience with the king of England. Albert Gallatin, who actually wrote much of the American Constitution while working for Thomas Jefferson, was originally from Geneva.

The church also had a defined role in the nation, teaching principles of justice and morality and calling the people and the government to account if the principles were violated. In later centuries the church backed away from this role, and the accountability vacuum that was left has been filled in Western nations by the media.

Economists today know that any country that practices hard work, favors the family structure, has reasonable interest rates, and lives by systems of law and accountability will have prosperity. The economic level will start to rise within the first generation, as was the case in sixteenth-century Geneva. Now institutions such as the International Monetary Fund and the World Bank teach these principles to the nations, but it was Calvin who first took these biblical teachings and applied them in a more modern context.

What happened in sixteenth-century Geneva was really about teaching the nations how they should live, which illustrates the difference between revival and reformation. In revival, lots of people get saved, new churches are started, and the Christians get committed. But revival often stops there.

In reformation, the same first steps of conversions, church planting, and commitment take place. But then someone realizes that people don't know how to live by biblical truths and need to be taught. They examine every part of the life of the nation to see what could be a biblical alternative to the cultural way of doing things.

John Calvin was not just a theologian. He studied and taught theology in order to rebuild the nation, so he was essentially an apostolic nation builder. He forged a biblical worldview, not because he liked to discuss philosophical issues but so that his adopted nation would survive. Calvin, like the apostle Paul, was also a missionary. Missionaries who are interested in completely accomplishing the will of God will be committed not just to saving souls, crucial as that is as a first step, but to teaching the nation. People who are actually doing the work of God in the nations often write the best theology.

Calvin was a master communicator and effectively used the technology of the day. He preached weekly in the cathedral and also taught daily in the former chapel next to it about the biblical instructions for every area of life. All over Europe, people were grappling with the same questions they faced in Geneva and were looking for ways to live out biblical truths. There was such continent-wide interest in what he taught that a scribe would sit in his class and take notes and afterward would take them directly to Calvin's printer. The notes would be typeset, printed, and on their way around Europe within the week. We can hardly publish this quickly today, even with computers and the internet! Calvin and his team were completely committed to teaching the nations.

The towns and villages 'round about were also asking Calvin and Farel to send pastors and teachers so they could start to live the Reformation. But there was nobody to send. Calvin's lieutenant, another Frenchman named Theodore de Beze (or "Beza" in some English histories), had started a training academy for pastors in Lausanne, but there was a split, and part of that academy was moved to Geneva in 1559. Calvin taught young ministers in training from an alcove in the chapel. Renamed "Calvin's Auditorium," it remained the place of the training of the future ministers of Geneva for two centuries. It was the birthplace of

the University of Geneva.

The Rise of the Sacred/Secular Divide

When Calvin and the French apostolic team came to Geneva in the sixteenth century, a powerful teaching was forged in the Spirit. But three generations after the death of the apostolic leadership, the Protestant church started to become more and more formalized, cold, and dead. Injustice was first tolerated and then institutionalized as political power fell back into the hands of a few families. Education was available only for the children of the well-off, and the poor went hungry. Some of the same trends happened in the Protestant church that had happened in the Catholic Church centuries earlier: It lost its purity and power.

The Enlightenment, a new movement that is with us today, began at that time as history repeated itself. Faced with the corruption of the church, people were again actively looking for a new way to live. When the church abdicated its role of teaching the nations, others picked up that mantle. The Enlightenment was brought on by a set of specific teachings, as a few men and women decided that the nations needed new teaching, a new Light. The Enlightenment shaped the faith of the church for generations. Not only were the nations taught from Geneva, but the church in the nations was also taught from that city.

One of the principal fathers of the Enlightenment was the French philosopher Voltaire. He often came to Geneva because it was the location of the workshop of his printer. After he was exiled from Paris, he bought a chateau just outside of Geneva. During the twenty years he lived there, his home was known as the intellectual capital of Europe.

Under his influence, the church accepted the teachings of the Enlightenment, including that the supernatural does not exist, miracles don't happen, Jesus Christ was not really divine, and the Bible was not really inspired. Humans could and should discover truth without divine help, science was the new religion that would save humanity, and peace and prosperity depended on human efforts alone. God, then, was no longer really necessary, except as a distant, impersonal First Cause who got things going and then withdrew from the earth. The idea that the church should worry only about the souls of people instead of about every aspect of their lives and society came from the influence of Enlightenment thought on the church.[1]

In Geneva, we see an important warning to heed: The church tries to speak to the culture and then, in learning the language, accommodates the culture, before finally becoming captive to it. This is a lesson we must heed today; in our efforts to be "seeker friendly," we must not lose our mandate to shape the culture instead of being shaped by it.

Reaction to the ordered, disciplined rationalism of the Enlightenment came quickly in the form of romanticism, or elevating experience over reason as our ultimate method of knowing reality. In the second wave of French Protestant refugees, a clockmaker named Rousseau arrived in Geneva and had a son named Jean-Jacques. Jean-Jacques reacted strongly against the church of his time, and against any idea of law or sin.

It was no coincidence that Rousseau was born and lived the early part of his life one street away from what had been Calvin's house. He took up the mantle

Calvin had created for teaching the nations. Rousseau is still one who teaches the teachers of the world. In practically any nation, including in Asia, you cannot become a school teacher unless you read what Rousseau said about teaching children.

The Romantic movement, fathered by Rousseau and others, still strongly influences the church today. The ideas that the church is there for my self-fulfillment, that my experience of God is the most fundamental reality in life, and that whatever is spontaneous is more spiritual than what is planned, come straight from Rousseau's teaching. He also taught that we are not really sinners but that our problems come from our environment, specifically the structures and institutions of society. When we are surprised at sin among Christians, we demonstrate that we are more influenced by Rousseau than by biblical truths.

This war of ideas in the eighteenth century highlights the fact that there are essentially two ways of knowing, whatever the worldview, world religion, or culture: the rationalist and the romantic. Jesus warned against these two temptations, represented by the Sadducees and the Pharisees (see Mark 8 and Matthew 16). Sadly, these two views are still foundational to much of our Christian theology today, even though Jesus warned us about these faulty beliefs two thousand years ago.

The romantic temptation (of the Pharisees) is to believe that God's power is submitted to my desires for health, wealth, and prosperity. The rationalist temptation (of the Sadducees) is to believe that God and His ways are subject to my reason. As the eighteenth century progressed, these two ways of thinking were taught through art, music, architecture, and philosophy and concentrated and diffused through the university systems, which powerfully discipled the nations and the church. Geneva was one of the high places for the transmission of these teachings to the nations.

In the theological corruption of the eighteenth century, a student could study in Calvin's academy to be a Protestant pastor for three years and never read the Bible (except when Hebrew was studied or a few psalms would be assigned). For three years students would learn Greek and Roman philosophy. The whole church was filled with the influence of rationalist, Enlightenment philosophy; in the early nineteenth century a Bible was published in Geneva that, like the Jehovah's Witness bible today, changed the references to Jesus Christ as the Son of God.

The changes in thinking were reflected in architecture itself. Under the influence of Greek philosophy, in the late eighteenth century a neoclassical portico with Greek columns was added to the cathedral where Calvin had preached.

In 1815 a young Scotsman named Robert Haldane came to Geneva. After visiting for just a few days, he walked around the city with a theology student prior to departing. This young man was getting ready to become a Protestant pastor. As Haldane spent the day with him, he was appalled at his lack of knowledge of the Bible and the absence of relationship with God. Haldane decided to stay, rented an apartment in the Old Town, and started holding Bible studies.

He invited the theology students to come, and they were very interested because they had never been to a Bible study. He found out later that most of them had never even read the epistle to the Romans! They started to get converted, and then some of their professors did as well. Revival started right in Geneva. Hundreds of people were saved, and then thousands as revival went into the neighboring canton of Vaud.

Some of these new converts stayed in the Reformed Church, and others started new churches. These are still called the Free Churches of Geneva. These churches had an incredible vision for missions. For example, they had a plan to reach every town, village, and farmhouse in France from Geneva. They would recruit farmers from the Jura Mountains who couldn't work in the winter, fill their backpacks with New Testaments, and send them door-to-door in France. They visited every house in France. They also sold a calendar that had agricultural advice and a Bible verse on it for every day. France in the nineteenth century knew the Bible better than France of the twentieth century because of the revival that started in Geneva and then went into France. Also, many of the missions to the French-speaking countries of Africa and the Pacific were begun through Geneva.

One young man, Henri Dunant, from the principal church of the revival, seemed to be mostly interested in making money. He often organized investment schemes, going to North Africa to try to find mines that people could invest in. As he was coming back from one of these trips, he visited a field covered with wounded and dead soldiers from a battle that had just taken place between the French and Austrian armies. He was told that if anyone went out to try to help or even bury them, they would be shot at by the other side. He decided to do something about it, so he gave his testimony about that visit in the revival church.

He also published a pamphlet, *A Visit to Solferino*, which pricked the conscience of Europe. Henri and some of his friends founded an organization that later became the International Red Cross. A few years afterward they called the nations to Geneva, where the 16 greatest powers at that time signed the treaty we know as the Geneva Convention.

This treaty is based on the biblical principles in the first part of the Book of Amos, which show that God is very concerned with the just conduct of war, and especially the righteous treatment of prisoners. The reason we are prosecuting war criminals from Serbia today is that the nations were taught from Geneva in this area. Sadly, this was the only area in which the revival of Geneva produced teaching for the nations.

In terms of influence on Swiss laws, the Reformation has a bigger impact even today than the revival ever did, though the Reformation happened almost three centuries before the revival. In giving us the Great Commission, Jesus said that there must be individual conversions (Mark 16:15) and that this should lead to discipling the nations (Matthew 28:20), so revival alone accomplishes only half of the task He entrusted to us. Apostolic leadership must take the zeal of new converts and teach them the implications of their faith in every area of their personal lives and the spheres of society in which they serve.

Revivals happen regularly in the history of the church; true reformation is a costly and lengthy process, so perhaps this is why it is so rare. It may be that the enemy so feared another Reformation in Geneva in the nineteenth century that he took very specific steps to bottle up the revival by bringing in the Enlightenment teachings. Under this influence, the revived church did not believe that it had much to say about government, poverty, or injustice. The church retreated, leaving a vacuum for the teaching of the nations. (See Vishal Mangalwadi's book *Carey in India* for a fascinating study of the Reformation-oriented pioneer mission work of William Carey and the first wave of missionaries to India, who were inspired by the teachings of the French Reformation out of Geneva. Mangalwadi contrasts this first wave of missions, which changed the history of India, with the more revival-oriented second wave, which in his opinion was not nearly as effective.)

Adding to this, a new teaching in the church said that there is going to be a Rapture at any minute, so believers must be sure they are ready and try to save all the souls they can. These are good teachings, but if absolutized they can lead to Christians not being concerned about the affairs of the nation. The believers of that day withdrew from the universities, from political life, and especially from the media. Years later they were amazed that all these vacancies had been filled with pagans.

Geneva continued to hold the mantle of anointing to teach the nations. Early in the twentieth century, a young revolutionary came to study in the city. He spent two years studying and writing in the University of Geneva library.

Much of the organization and preparation for his revolution took place there. In the process he picked up the mantle of the teaching of the nations.

His name was Vladimir Ilyich Lenin. Until 1989, 80 percent of the world's population was being taught by his ideas, known as the Marxist-Leninist system. It was not a very intelligent system, and it didn't work very well. But it was unified and coherent, and any country could adopt it. It told his adherents what to do about their schools, economy, army, and political system—about every area of life. Nations on every continent adopted this system because there wasn't any better system as an alternative.

In one generation, Geneva was transformed. What can we learn from its story on the vital subject of nation discipling?

The church responded to the moral and spiritual vacuum of the day with gospel preaching to bring individual conversion over an entire generation. This was coupled with intentional teaching on how to live the Christian faith in every area of life and society.

The church prayed and searched the Scriptures for biblical truths to shape every sphere of society and proactively brought this teaching and moral accountability to the leaders in every area. The church did not hide in its buildings. It was a very robust presence throughout the city.

Church leaders, together with their counterparts from other nations, continued to seek God on what God was doing around the world in this area of discipling every area of life in His ways. The church was deeply committed to the poor, caring for immediate physical needs and training in skills to enable the needy to live godly, self-sufficient lives.

To reap all the benefit from a study of Geneva's story, we must also take an honest look at the mistakes that were made so we can work to avoid them in the future. One category of error had to do with crossing the biblical lines of authority, or domains. Every conflict in society can be traced back to the question of domains: Who has the right to make the decisions in this area? In Geneva, several examples illustrate this important principle:

Neighborhood tribunals were intended to help disciple families. Instead, they demonstrated the negative effects of the church overstepping its bounds and exercising an inappropriate degree of authority in people's lives.

One tribunal punished an individual because he wouldn't convert, publicly disqualifying him from a leadership role in another sphere. These actions highlight two areas of error. The church is to be an influence for salvation; it must not exert control over the personal right to choose. The church has a teaching role but is not to exercise direct control over the other spheres of society.

There was also a rigidity in applying scriptural principles, which led to legalism on external issues such as dress or leisure time activities. Also, the church focused almost exclusively on the application of biblical truths to their city, demonstrating a poor understanding of missions and missing the opportunity to extend God's kingdom even more.

As the years went on after Calvin passed away, there was an over-intellectualism of the faith.

Although Calvin preached about the priesthood of every believer and detested the Catholic practice of looking to a priest for salvation, Calvin still left too much authority in the person of the Protestant pastor. For centuries afterward, pastors were still seen as the ones who could exclusively do ministry. This was not an avenue for every believer.

Today, the nations are looking for answers. Moreover, it is the commandment of Jesus Christ and the calling of the church to teach the nations. If we step back from this again, we will leave another vacuum.

Whenever the church leaves a vacuum, the enemy is very happy to fill it. He is probably working on another system for the nations even now. If it is like his other recent efforts, it will be a mixture of nationalism, racist scapegoating, economic hope, and fearmongering. But the next version might well include supernatural power, and it will be freed from the residual morality of modernity. It will not be nice.

Will the church be ready with an attractive, intelligent, biblical alternative? The lessons of Geneva will help those who rise up to take on this challenge.

Tom Bloomer, who wrote Chapter Seven, studied archaeology at the University of Illinois (BA 1972), and worked as a French translator, ladies' shoe salesman, and youth pastor before joining Youth With A Mission. After attending the School of Evangelism in 1974 in Lausanne, Tom and his wife, Cynthia, joined YWAM's French Ministries, led that work for several years, and then became base leaders at Lausanne. In 1983 they responded to a call from Loren Cunningham and Howard Malmstadt to help develop the University of the Nations (UofN). A master's degree in missiology from Wheaton (1987) and years of cross-cultural experience proved invaluable as Tom helped coordinate, refine, and improve the different courses developing through the UofN. Tom completed a PhD in Theology of Education at Trinity International University in 1999 and served as the International Provost of the UofN from 2001–2018. He is now Provost Emeritus.

Teaching the Word is the primary thrust of Tom's ministry; the challenge before him is to discover what it means to love God not just with our heart, soul, and strength but with our minds as well. Tom's book, *Cinderella and Her Sisters; Identity, Authority, and Inheritance*, was published in French in 2016 and in English in 2018. The English version is available on Amazon, in both paperback and Kindle versions.

Tom is International Provost Emeritus at YWAM's University of the Nations. He blogs at Education, Gardening and Life (*tombloomer.com*).

University of the Nations, *uofn.edu*; *facebook.com/UniversityoftheNations*.

Acknowledgments

First, my thanks to friends and fellow educators Dr. Robert Osburn of The Wilberforce Academy, Dr. Christian Overman of Worldview Matters, and Dr. Elizabeth Youmans of Chrysalis International. These friends have a common interest in the relationship of the intersection of worldview and education, and they all have a passion for people, particularly in the global south, having access to an education philosophy and pedagogy that will build nations of freedom.

Thanks, also, to the contributors to this book, Scott and Kimberly Allen, Thomas Bloomer, Vishal Mangalwadi, Christian Overman, and Elizabeth Youmans. Thank you for your vision and your passion for ideas and the kind of education that is transformative of children, families, and nations. Thank you for making your contributions to this compendium. I trust that this book will provide access to a greater audience for the ideas you have so graciously shared.

My thanks to editors and friends, Gary Brumbelow and Stan Guthrie, who have helped with both substantive and copyediting of this book. Without their efforts, this book would never have seen the light of day.

Also, thank you too to Scott Allen, the President of the Disciple Nations Alliance. Scott and I have enjoyed years of talking and thinking together. Scott has a sharp, penetrating, and analytical mind. "Iron sharpening iron" marks our relationship and stimulates a rich engagement into the writing process.

My thanks to Viviana Velie, a good friend and the Director of JUCUM Publishing house, our Spanish publisher. Thank you for your advice and enthusiastic encouragement for the books that we are writing.

Thanks to Tim Beals and the team at Credo House Publishing for your vision for and work on this book. It is so good to partner with you on this project.

Most of all, thanks to my wife, Marilyn, who is my best friend and life's adventuresome companion for over half a century. Thank you, Marilyn, for your patience and support as I continue to write and speak.

Introduction to the Study Guide

This study guide is designed to help you reflect on and apply what you are reading in *Schooling versus Education*. It is intended for both individuals and small groups.

How to Use This Guide

Before you read each section of the book, take time to pray and ask the Holy Spirit to be your teacher. Then read through the study guide for that section; sometimes there are questions to be answered before the reading. You can answer the remaining questions either as you are reading or after you have finished.

Although *Schooling versus Education* has seven chapters, this study guide has 22 sessions to enable you to thoroughly absorb what you are learning. You will see a marker SG in the margin at each point in the book that corresponds with a study guide section. When you come to that marker in your reading, stop there and review the study guide for that section.

In a small-group setting, we suggest a goal of reading and discussing one or two study guide sections each week. Take time to pray before you read to ask the Spirit of God to teach you. The purpose of education is to practice what is true. So, develop the habit of applying something that you have learned from each lesson.

Know and Do: A Word about Application

The ancient Greeks stressed *knowing*. They wanted to fill the mind with knowledge but had little interest in applying what they learned. The Hebrew people, on the other hand, were interested in both *knowing* and *doing* the truth. Today, many Christians, unfortunately, are more like ancient Greeks than Hebrews.

This is a sad commentary, given that wisdom is the moral application of truth, goodness, and beauty. This study guide will encourage you to develop a "Hebrew mind"—to apply what you have learned.

The Book of Proverbs, in the Old Testament, uses three words that are interrelated but not synonymous; they are distinct and hierarchal in significance. The words are *knowledge*, *wisdom*, and *understanding*. Each addresses a very different question. Examine what each means and the question it answers.

- Knowledge—the collection of data and information: What does it declare?
- Understanding—discernment, appending what is important: What does it mean?
- Wisdom—the moral application of truth: How do we apply it?

Each session in this study guide has two parts. In the sections marked "Know," you will be challenged with questions to help you reflect on what you have read. They will deal with two issues, knowledge (What does it declare?) and understanding (What does it mean?).

The sections marked "Do" will encourage you to put into practice at least one thing you have learned during that week's study.

This study guide will help you to reflect more deeply on the material in the book. It will also help group leaders to guide the discussion about the book.

You will find many open-ended questions. They will help you to think through the reading and frame what you are learning personally. Use conceptual learning, not rote learning, to test your own understanding and to think ahead about what you will do with this new knowledge and understanding.

Here is the content of the study guide:

- SESSION: Introduction
- SESSION 1a: Schooling versus Education
- SESSION 1b: Hidden and Discovered
- SESSION 1c: *Veritas*
- SESSION 1d: Drifting into Danger
- SESSION 1e: Encyclopedia
- SESSION 1f: Eupraxia
- SESSION 2a: The Christian View of Children
- SESSION 2b: Biblical Principles That Undergird the Christian View of Children
- SESSION 3a: The Remarkable Role of the Bible in Early American Education

- SESSION 3b: Christ-Centered Education Produces Leaders
- SESSION 3c: The American Revolution Was Fueled by Preaching
- SESSION 3d: Teaching Character and Understanding at Home
- SESSION 4a: Seminary: Education or Religious Schooling?
- SESSION 4b: Fragmentation of Knowledge: From Modernism to Post-modernism
- SESSION 5a: Why Education? The Lost Purpose for Learning
- SESSION 5b: The Lost Idea of "The Whole"
- SESSION 5c: There's No Room on Christ's Throne for Two
- SESSION 5d: Earth-Tending Is God's Assignment for Human Beings
- SESSION 6: Home Education
- SESSION 7a: John Calvin in Geneva: A Nation-Building Missionary
- SESSION 7b: The Rise of the Sacred/Secular Divide

Please note that SG in the margin of a chapter identifies the place within the text for which the study guide has been developed.

May God richly bless you as you process the material in *Schooling versus Education*.

Darrow L. Miller
Co-founder, Disciple Nations Alliance

Study Guide

SESSION: Introduction

KNOW:

- **Knowledge**—What does it declare?
  - » Before you begin, take a moment to reflect on your understanding of the difference between schooling and education.
  - » What does the section say about language and culture-shaping education?
  - » What was the religion upon which the United States was founded?
  - » What is the religion that the nation is built upon today?
- **Understanding**—What does it mean?
  - » What kind of society do you want to live in, a free society or a society of tyranny and absolute power? Why?
  - » If you want to live in a free society, why do you need to think seriously about your education or the education of your children or grandchildren?
  - » Paraphrase, in your own words, Mark Fakkema's quotation.
  - » What is the "operative" worldview or sacred belief system of your culture?
  - » How has this impacted the educational philosophy and system in your country?

DO:

- **Wisdom**—How do we apply it?
  - » How will you begin to function differently based on your understanding that language and culture shape education?
  - » First Peter 1:13 states: "Therefore, preparing your minds for action, and being sober-minded, set your hope fully on the grace that will be brought to you at the revelation of Jesus Christ." In light of the importance of education for building up people to live in freedom, what will you DO to "prepare your mind for action"?

SESSION 1a: Schooling versus Education

KNOW:

- **Knowledge**—What does this section declare?
  - » What does the Bible (Genesis 1:26–28) reveal about the nature of human beings?
  - » What is the cultural mandate? What are the twin subordinating principles?
  - » List the four principles derived from Christ's teaching on the pursuit of truth in John 8:31–32.
  - » In Acts 17:11, Luke writes: "Now [the Berean Jews] were more noble than those in Thessalonica; they received the message with all eagerness, examining the Scriptures daily to see if [the things Paul said] were true." What distinguishes each group?
- **Understanding**—What does it mean?
  - » The Bible and creation are clear: There is a God beyond the universe. He has created human beings for a purpose. If there were no God in the universe, what would be the implications for human identity and purpose?
  - » What are the implications of this truth for our world today? From which orientation do you function?
  - » State in your own words the implications of each of the four principles in the pursuit of truth.
  - » What is the relationship between the pursuit of truth and the pursuit of freedom?
  - » What are the implications of this for education?
  - » In 2016 the Oxford Dictionaries (OD) declared that we are living in a post-truth culture. Postmodern culture no longer believes in truth. What are the implications of this new era for education? And for free societies?

DO:

- **Wisdom**—How do we apply it?
  - » Thinking of the distinction between the character of the Thessalonians and of the Bereans, which one is characteristic of your life (not what you want it to be, but what it is)? Does your pastor want the congregation to be full of people who ask questions and pursue truth? What do tyrannical governments want in this regard?

- » Based on your reflection, identify one way in which you will promote the pursuit of truth in one of the following areas: your life, your church, in society, or in education.

SESSION 1b: Hidden and Discovered

KNOW:

- **Knowledge**—What does this section declare?
    - » What is the fount of science?
    - » What does creation communicate?
    - » What are the three books that the educational reformers identified as the source of God's revelation?
- **Understanding**—What does it mean?
    - » What does it mean that truth is discovered and not created?
    - » What is Jacques Monod's "profound epistemological contradiction"?
    - » Why does this contradiction exist for atheistic scientists? Why does it not exist for theists?
    - » Why did many early scientists see no dichotomy between science and faith?
    - » Why does such a divorce exist in society today? In church today?
    - » What are the implications of the three books for education today?

DO:

- **Wisdom**—How do we apply it?
    - » What does it mean for you, personally, that truth is discovered and not created? What does this mean in terms of your thought life and the words you use?
    - » Reflect on your own life. What has been, to this point, its fount of truth?
    - » In light of what you have learned, list the top two or three things that will need to change in your life.

SESSION 1c: *Veritas*

KNOW:

- **Knowledge**—What does this section declare?
    - » The Reformers and their historical children, the Puritans, had a comprehensive view of education, known as *technologia*. What were the three elements of this theology of education?
    - » List five things you have learned from the Harvard shield.
- **Understanding**—What does it mean?
    - » What is the relationship between the three books and the pursuit of truth?
    - » What is the meaning of Comenius's concept of erecting temples of wisdom?
    - » Jesus said that truth will set you free. If you want to live in a free society, what is the importance of having a biblical theology of education?
    - » The first universities in North America were founded on the theology of education known as *technologia*. Describe the original purpose of these educational institutions.
    - » Dr. Georgia Purdom describes the erosion of the Harvard shield as Western societies have moved from a theistic foundation to an atheistic foundation. Describe this erosion in your own words.
    - » Why will a nation founded on atheistic principles not remain free?

DO:

- **Wisdom**—How do we apply it?
    - » How can you begin to create "temples of wisdom" through your own life? What can/will you do to contribute to the building of culture in your community through your vocation?
    - » If you want your children and grandchildren to live in a free society, what will you do to work toward an educational system built on the principles of *technologia*?

SESSION 1d: Drifting into Danger

KNOW:

- **Knowledge**—What does this section declare?
  - » What has replaced the biblical worldview?
  - » With what has the church replaced the biblical worldview?
- **Understanding**—What does this mean?
  - » State the logical consequences of this shift for society in general and for education in particular.
  - » Summarize the relationship between reason and revelation in each of the four quadrants of the diagram.
  - » What are the implications of each quadrant?
  - » Explain evangelical gnosticism.
  - » How has this groomed young Christians to enter the irrational realm of postmodernism?

DO:

- **Wisdom**—How do we apply it?
  - » Reflect on your own experience. Where do you see the sacred/secular dichotomy in your church? In your life?
  - » What steps can you take to pursue biblical orthodoxy?
  - » What steps can you take to encourage the restoration of a biblical theology of education?

SESSION 1e: Encyclopedia

KNOW:

- **Knowledge**—What does this section declare?
  - » What is the root concept of "university"?
  - » What does the word *encyclopedia* mean?
  - » What are the four key elements of the circle of knowledge?
- **Understanding**—What does this mean?
  - » What are the implications of the compound words for university? What are the implications for education that leads to freedom?
  - » Today we have "diversities," not "universities." State what this means in terms of one's education and the fragmentation of societies.

- » Describe the interplay among the key elements of the circle of knowledge and the culmination of your life bringing glory to God.
- » According to the Puritan vision for education:
  - ◊ What are the key elements?
  - ◊ What do these produce in people? In society?

DO:

- **Wisdom**—How do we apply it?
  - » How might you begin a discussion among your friends or within your church about re-forming the educational philosophy and system in your community?

SESSION 1f: Eupraxia

KNOW:

- **Knowledge**—What does this section declare?
  - » What is the meaning of the word *eupraxia*?
  - » What is the meaning of the Hebrew word a*vodah*?
  - » What is the heart of the distinction between the French and American Revolutions?
  - » What did the Reformers seek to reform?
- **Understanding**—What does it mean?
  - » Describe the *Protestant work ethic.* How does this ethic create nations of freedom?
  - » What was the role of the church in society during the Protestant Reformation? In education? Does today's church see this as her role? If not, how is the situation different?
  - » How does the concept of governance relate to the concept of discipling nations?
  - » Describe the relationship between eupraxia and *avodah*?
  - » What is the role of education in the shaping of a nation?

DO:

- **Wisdom**—How do we apply it?
  - » List the five most important concepts you have read about education in this section.

  - » Why are these important to you?
  - » What one thing will you do to apply one of these insights in your own life and community?

SESSION 2a: The Christian View of Children

KNOW:

- **Knowledge**—What does this section declare?
  - » What is the state of children in:
    - ◊ The world (list five realities)?
    - ◊ The church (list five realities)?
  - » List the eight principles that lay the foundation for the Christian view of the child.
- **Understanding**—What does it mean?
  - » Who is primarily responsible for the education of children—parents or the state? Why?
  - » In your nation, who is considered responsible for the education of children? In your church, who is considered responsible? What are the implications of this?
  - » Which two of the eight principles that lay the foundation for the Christian view of the child are the most impactful for you to understand? Why?

DO:

- **Wisdom**—How do we apply it?
  - » Understanding the significance of the eight principles, pick one that you will consciously and concretely apply.
  - » What will you do? When will you do it? Who will you ask to hold you accountable?

SESSION 2b: Biblical Principles That Undergird the Christian View of Children

KNOW:

- **Knowledge**—What does this section declare?

- » List four of the principles of nurturing Christianly that seem most significant to you.
- **Understanding**—What does this mean?
  - » Paraphrase Rosalie J. Slater's poem, "I Am God's Workmanship."
  - » In the chart on the Two Educational Views of Children, reflect on one of the contrasts:
    - ◊ Why is it important to understand this particular distinction?
    - ◊ How would you rate your own educational experience or that of your children or grandchildren in this area?
  - » Dr. Youmans speaks of every child having "internal property."
    - ◊ What does this mean?
    - ◊ How is this to be nurtured?
  - » What are the implications of this for the discipling of nations (the Great Commission, Mathew 28:18–20)?

DO:

- **Wisdom**—How do we apply it?
  - » Which view of education, the traditional or the transformational, have you held?
  - » Has your conviction changed? Why or why not?
  - » What will you do differently because of your view?

SESSION 3a: The Remarkable Role of the Bible in Early American Education

KNOW:

- **Knowledge**—What does this section declare?
  - » What was one of the main concerns that led the Pilgrims and Puritans to leave Europe for the New World?
  - » Whom did they believe bore responsibility for their children's education?
  - » Where were children educated in the colonial period?
  - » What notations in the Geneva Bible were so threatening to King James I, and why?
  - » According to Dr. Youmans, what is the most important principle for building a Christian culture?

- **Understanding**—What does this mean?
  - » Someone coined the phrase the "protestant *word* ethic."
    - ◊ Why are words so important?
    - ◊ Why did Noah Webster create his own dictionary of American English?
    - ◊ What role do words play in fulfilling the Great Commission of discipling nations?
    - ◊ What happens when a culture abandons words for images?
  - » What is the meaning of the term *self-government*?
  - » If people of a nation are not self-governing, who will govern them?
  - » How are self-governing people developed?
  - » Paraphrase Noah Webster's quote about the Bible, Christian virtue, and education creating a free society.
  - » If your society is not free or is becoming less free, what is likely the root of this? What are the implications in the area of education?

DO:

- **Wisdom**—How do we apply it?
  - » Pick one of the following applications:
    - ◊ In what area(s) do you need to improve in becoming a self-governing person? How can you begin to do better?
    - ◊ Reflecting on the relationship of the Word of God to a free society, what one thing will you do to begin to ground or re-ground education in your community in the Word of God?

SESSION 3b: Christ-Centered Education Produces Leaders

KNOW:

- **Knowledge**—What does this section declare?
  - » Where does the first call for education appear in the Bible?
  - » What single book had the most important cultural and political influence in the formation of the United States as a free and self-governing nation, and why?
- **Understanding**—What does this mean?

» Describe the ways in which the Bible helped to shape the experiment in freedom known as the United States.
» What are the consequences of atheistic, secular, state-sponsored education in nations today?
» Dr. Youmans states the impact that social media and distance learning via computers has had on education and the minds of children. Summarize in your own words what this has cost us.
» Paraphrase the purpose of education revealed by Webster's 1828 definition of that word.
» Describe what Dr. Youmans has sought to produce after reading Benjamin Rush's essay on education. What is your reaction to what she has described?

DO:

- **Wisdom**—How do we apply it?
    » Identify one of the ideas you have just read that is inspiring to you. Develop a creative response to what has impacted you. Create a podcast or video, or write an essay that you can share with others.

SESSION 3c: The American Revolution Was Fueled by Preaching

KNOW:

- **Knowledge**—What does this section declare?
    » In colonial times there were no public schools as we know them today. List the ways in which children were educated.
    » What was the role of the pulpit in early American education?
- **Understanding**—What does it mean?
    » Describe the kinds and scope of preaching in colonial America.
    » Describe the impact this pulpit ministry had on the formation of the nation.
    » Historian George Bancroft wrote: "The American Revolution was but the application of the principles of the Reformation to civil government."
        ◊ What did he mean by that?
        ◊ What did this preaching lead to?
    » To what does the "Pulpit of the Revolution" refer?

- » As the new nation was founded and wholistic teaching from the pulpits in America began to shift to an exclusively spiritual kind of preaching, what began to replace the pulpit in the education of the nation's children? Explain.

DO:

- **Wisdom**—How do we apply it?
  - » Compare and contrast the educational impact of the colonial era, with the pulpit, family, and home involved educationally, in shaping the nation with the impact of the public school and the teacher's desk in shaping the world today. What conclusions do you draw? How will this shape your being an educational reformer?

SESSION 3d: Teaching Character and Understanding at Home

KNOW:

- **Knowledge**—What does this segment declare?
  - » What was first taught in the home? List some of the virtues that were taught by the parents to their children:
  - » Where were the foundations of self-government laid and practiced?
- **Understanding**—What does this mean?
  - » If a nation is to be free, her citizens need to be self-governing. If people are not self-governing, they are lawless. What are the consequences for a nation? Where do you see these consequences in your own nation?
  - » Pick some of the highlights of John and Abigail Adams's commitment to homeschooling with regard to their children's education.
  - » What is your reflective response to their modeling for their progeny?
  - » Reread the last paragraph of this paper. What did colonial education produce? What is your response to this outcome?

DO:

- **Wisdom**—How do we apply it?
  - » What is the lawlessness you see in your own nation?

- » For people to be self-governing, they need to be taught biblical principles and virtues. Do you see these being taught in your own country? If you do, how might you support this effort? If you do not see biblical principles and virtues being taught, where and how can you begin?

SESSION 4a: Seminary: Education or Religious Schooling?

KNOW:

- **Knowledge**—What does this section declare?
  - » William Carey was a missionary living in an era in which Christians functioned from a biblical worldview. Make a list of
    - ◊ What Carey did.
    - ◊ What Carey taught.
  - » List the three books on the Harvard Crest.
  - » List some of the Christians who helped to establish the framework for the American educational philosophy and system.
  - » As a theologian, Galileo studied the Word of God. Which passages informed his decision to challenge the ruling paradigm of the church and the pope?
- **Understanding**—What does it mean?
  - » Today we think of missionaries as doing "spiritual" work, i.e., evangelism, church planting, and discipling in "spiritual" things. Why might Carey and other missionaries of his generation have had a broader agenda?
  - » Describe each of the three books on the Harvard Crest. What did each reveal? How did they relate to one another?
  - » Why and how has Christianity lost America?
  - » What is the relation between God's Word and reason? Why are both important?
  - » How did Galileo, a theologian and a scientist, challenge the church and the pope?
  - » We usually think in terms of God's revelation. How has God *concealed* things? Why?

DO:

- **Wisdom**—How do we apply it?

» Write a poem, essay, blog, or newspaper article describing the three books and why it is essential to restore them as the foundation of education.

SESSION 4b: Fragmentation of Knowledge: From Modernism to Postmodernism

KNOW:

- **Knowledge**—What does this section declare?
  - » Why did C. S. Lewis say he believed "in Christianity as I believe in the rising sun"?
- **Understanding**—What does this mean?
  - » What does the phrase "theology is the queen of science" mean?
  - » How did the use of the God-given gift of reason become mere rationalism?
  - » What happened when modern "Christians" began to accept the assumptions of evolutionism and reject the authority of Scripture over humanity?
  - » What happened when "fundamentalist" Christians rebelled against modernism and rejected reason?
  - » Describe what postmodernism has done to today's universities in terms of the "silo-ing" of knowledge.
  - » How did the Bible school and seminary concepts of education contribute to the disintegration of today's universities?

DO:

- **Wisdom**—How do we apply it?
  - » What is the most important thing about education that you have learned from Vishal Mangalwadi's chapter?
  - » How will this impact how you contribute to reforming education? Be specific.

SESSION 5a: Why Education? The Lost Purpose for Learning

KNOW:

- **Knowledge**—What does this section declare?

   - » When were the seeds planted to secularize the nation and privatize faith?
   - » Explain the concept of the sacred/secular divide.
- **Understanding**—What does it mean?
   - » How do you respond to the A. A. Hodge quote?
   - » An atheistic, anti-theistic faith is at the foundation of state-sponsored education, the chapter says. What are the consequences?
   - » Where do you see the residue of dualistic thinking in your own life? In your church?
   - » How are even "Christian" schools impacted by the SSD? How do they contribute to producing Christians who are dualists?
   - » List some basic questions a parent or grandparent might ask teachers and administrators to ascertain whether dualism exists in a school?

DO:

- **Wisdom**—How do we apply it?
   - » Have you assumed that state-sponsored education is "neutral"?
   - » If you have, take some time to reflect on what the revelations in this section have meant in your life and in the lives of your children and/or grandchildren. How will this insight impact you going forward?
   - » Write down a brief plan to help others in your circle see that state-sponsored education has a destructive agenda to shape the minds of children. This may be as simple as inviting them to read this book.

SESSION 5b: The Lost Idea of "The Whole"

KNOW:

- **Knowledge**—What does this section declare?
   - » What concept was lost when the Bible was abandoned by society?
   - » What does the Bible (Genesis 1:26–28) declare to be the purpose for humankind's existence on the earth?
- **Understanding**—What does it mean?
   - » Describe why the loss of the whole matters.

- » Describe the distinction Dr. Erik Strandness makes in declaring that God created not *ex nihilo* (out of nothing) but *ex cōgitātiō* (out of thought). Do you agree or disagree? Why?
- » What is the Cultural Mandate?
- » How can education help prepare children to govern when they are adults?

DO:

- **Wisdom**—How do we apply it?
  - » What is included in your sphere of governance?
  - » List, specifically, five things you can do to build up your ability to govern. Which one can you begin today, and how?

SESSION 5c: There's No Room on Christ's Throne for Two

KNOW:

- **Knowledge**—What does this section declare?
  - » List the four ways the word *kosmos* is used in the New Testament.
  - » List the scope of earth-tending, as described by Dr. Overman.
- **Understanding**—What does this mean?
  - » How is the meaning of *kosmos* as a system of thought and behavior related to education?
  - » Paraphrase Dr. Overman's statement of distinction: "God is in absolute control, but He does not control all things absolutely." Do you find this distinction helpful? How?
  - » Paraphrase the concept and scope of human beings as stewards of creation.
  - » How does the Puritan concept of the Circle of Knowledge relate to education?

DO:

- **Wisdom**—How do we apply it?
  - » List four or five ways you might apply lessons from this section. Then pick one and "just do it."

SESSION 5d: Earth-Tending Is God's Assignment for Human Beings

KNOW:

- **Knowledge**—What does this section declare?
  - » According to Dr. Overman, what is the purpose of education? State it exactly.
  - » What gives life and education enduring meaning?
- **Understanding**—What does this mean?
  - » How has the sacred/secular divide in our thinking influenced your view of work/vocation? Your view of education?
  - » Before now, what has been your understanding of the Great Commission?
  - » How would you describe the Great Commission now?
  - » Pick one of the 25 promises of human flourishing that particularly resonates with you. Describe why it is meaningful for you.
  - » Describe how you would contextualize education within the big picture of the Cultural Commission and the Great Commission.

DO:

- **Wisdom**—How do we apply it?
  - » Do you agree with Dr. Overman's declared purpose of education?
    - ◊ If yes, how are you manifesting this purpose in your role as an educator?
    - ◊ If not, what would your proposed purpose statement be?

SESSION 6: Home Education

KNOW:

- **Knowledge**—What does this chapter declare?
  - » What are the Scripture passages that denote the relationship between parents and children?
  - » What is the integration point of state-sponsored education? Of home education?
  - » What are some of the barriers to home education?
- **Understanding**—What does it mean?

  - » Who has the primary responsibility for educating your children? Would you agree or disagree with the author's stance on this issue? Why?
  - » What does the term "factory education" imply? Is this a fair or unfair term? Why?
  - » Why is the integration point you choose for your child's education so important?
  - » What does state-sponsored education typically inculcate in children?
  - » How do you see this outcome manifest in your society?
  - » What are some of the advantages that you see in home education?

DO:

- If you have been convinced that education of children is more the responsibility of the parents than the state, what are one or two specific things you will do to encourage that in your family or community?

SESSION 7a: John Calvin in Geneva: A Nation-Building Missionary

KNOW:

- **Knowledge**—What does this section declare?
  - » Describe the city of Geneva before the Protestant Reformation.
  - » Describe Geneva after the Protestant Reformation.
  - » What did the Reformers understand about the nature of the Bible?
  - » What three things marked the Reformers' strategy in reforming a city and a nation?
- **Understanding**—What does this mean?
  - » What brought such dramatic change to Geneva?
  - » What kinds of questions were the people of Europe asking? What similarities do you see to the questions being asked today in your country?
  - » How did the church of Calvin's day answer people's questions? How does this compare with the church's answers today?
  - » How was the Reformation pulpit the place of teaching for the whole city? What was taught from the pulpit?
  - » How did the Reformation impact education?

DO:

- **Wisdom**—How do we apply it?
  - » Describe what wholistic education can contribute to the discipling of a city or a nation. Thinking of your role as a parent, teacher, school administrator, and so on, what expertise and experience can you bring to help this to happen in your community?

SESSION 7b: The Rise of the Sacred/Secular Divide

KNOW:

- **Knowledge**—What does this declare?
  - » When the church lost its vibrancy and its vision for the discipling of nations in the generations after the Reformation, what movements took over that task?
- **Understanding**—What does it mean?
  - » Describe Dr. Bloomer's description of the four-step process of the church becoming like the culture. What are the parallels with the church today?
  - » Describe the distinction between a revival and a reformation.
  - » Why do we tend to see more revivals than reformations?
  - » What, according to Bloomer, were some of the deficiencies that followed the Reformation?
  - » How do you see these deficiencies as still being operative in the church today?
  - » What is the role of the church in "teaching the nations"?

DO:

- **Wisdom**—How do we apply it?
  - » Many of our countries are at a turning point, as is the church. Bloomer ends his essay with, "Will the church be ready with an attractive, intelligent, biblical alternative?" What has this essay done to encourage you to take on this challenge?

Subject Index

Y

Z

Scripture Index

1 Peter

2 Peter

1 John

3 John

Revelation

Endnotes

Preface

1 The concept was originally attribute to Mark Twain, but the thought is expressed as early as 1894 in Grant Allen's book *Post-Prandial Philosophy,* where Allen states: "What a misfortune it is that we should thus be compelled to let our boy's schooling interfere with their education."

2 Youmans, Elizabeth. 2018. "Teaching, Learning and Changed Lives." *Darrow Miller and Friends.* http://darrowmillerandfriends.com/2018/06/18/teaching-learning-changed-lives/.

3 Webster, Noah. 1828. *American Dictionary of the English Language* (online edition). http://webstersdictionary1828.com/.

4 Harper, Douglas. 2019. *Online Etymology Dictionary.* https://www.etymonline.com/.

5 Milton, John. 1909–14. *Tractate on Education.* Vol. III, Part 4. The Harvard Classics. New York: P.F. Collier & Son. https://www.bartleby.com/3/4/1.html.

Introduction

1 See https://www.theatlantic.com/magazine/archive/2019/10/when-the-culture-war-comes-for-the-kids/596668/.

2 Ibid.

3 Solway, David. 2018. "The End of Education." *PJ Media.* https://pjmedia.com/trending/the-end-of-education/.

4 Christian Overman has produced a video called *Not Far Away* that describes how churches have separated the Word of God from an increasingly secularized educational approach, producing a debilitating dualism and the privatization of Christianity, even in so-called "Christian" schools. See Christian Overman, "Education, Scripture and the Church: The Big Disconnect," *Darrow Miller and Friends,* March 15, 2018, http://darrowmillerandfriends.com/2018/03/15/education-scripture-church-disconnect/.

5 Dunphy, John J. 1983. "A Religion For A New Age." *The Humanist.* https://medium.com/@johnjdunphy/a-religion-for-a-new-age-f812839c4cb8.

6 Prager, Dennis; video interview on *Just the News*; January 23, 2021 - https://justthenews.com/politics-policy/education/dennis-prager-save-america-lefts-destruction-take-your-kids-out-public.

7 Park, George Kerlin. 2020. "Animism." *Encyclopaedia Britannica*. https://www.britannica.com/topic/animism.

8 Cahill, Thomas. 1998. *The Gifts of the Jews*. New York: Nan A. Talese. 239–41.

9 Webster, Daniel. "Preface," *Webster's Dictionary* 1828 Online Edition. http://webstersdictionary1828.com/Preface.

10 Youmans, Elizabeth. 2018. "God's Word Creates Virtuous Nations," *Darrow Miller and Friends*. http://darrowmillerandfriends.com/2018/12/03/gods-word-creates-virtuous-nations/.

11 Youmans, Elizabeth. 2017. "The Role of the Bible in Early American Education," *Darrow Miller and Friends*. http://darrowmillerandfriends.com/2017/06/22/bible-role-early-american-education/.

12 Fakkema, Mark. 1954. *Christian Philosophy and Its Educational Implications*. Christian School Service Inc. 2.

13 Webster, Noah. 1828. *American Dictionary of the English Language*. Online Edition. http://webstersdictionary1828.com/Quotes.

Chapter One

1 The Bible Project. "The Image of God." https://thebibleproject.com/explore/image-god/.

2 The Bible Project, *op. cit.*

3 Kuyper, Abraham. *Sphere Sovereignty*. Quoted in Bratt, James D., ed. 1998. *Abraham Kuyper: A Centennial Reader*. Grand Rapids: Eerdmans.

4 For more on this, see *Discipling Nations: The Power of Truth to Transform Culture* by Darrow L. Miller, with Stan Guthrie.

5 Leeden, Michael. 2018. "The Anti-American Americans," *PJ Media*. https://pjmedia.com/michaelledeen/the-anti-american-americans/.

6 Swanson, James. 1997. *Dictionary of Biblical Languages with Semantic Domains: Hebrew (Old Testament)*. Oak Harbor: Logos.

7 Monod, Jacques. 1971. *Chance and Necessity*. New York: Knopf. 21–22.

8 Christianity Today. 2000. "Francis Bacon: Philosopher of science," *Christian History*. https://www.christianitytoday.com/history/people/scholarsandscientists/francis-bacon.html.

9 "Frases de famosos." https://citas.in/frases/1923920-aristotle-plato-is-dear-to-me-but-dearer-still-is-truth/.

10 Hilmar-Jezek, Kytha. 2016. "The Father of Modern Education," *Tres Bohemes*. http://www.tresbohemes.com/2016/08/father-of-modern-education/.

11 See Gibbs, Lee W. 1971. "The Puritan Natural Law Theory of William Ames," *Harvard Theological Reviewi*. 37–57. https://www.cambridge.org/core/journals/harvard-theological-review/article/the-puritan-natural-law-theory-of-william-ames/9962AC3D9689710B5866A6778825EE22.

12 "Johann Heinrich Alsted," *Wikipedia*. https://en.wikipedia.org/wiki/Johann_Heinrich_Alsted.

13 Scott, David Hill. "A Vision of Veritas: What Christian Scholarship Can Learn from the Puritan's [*sic*] 'Technology' of Integrating Truth," *LeadershipU*, http://www.leaderu.com/aip/docs/scott.html.

14 Ibid.

15 "Shield and 'Veritas' History," Harvard GSAS Christian Community. http://www.hcs.harvard.edu/~gsascf/shield-and-veritas-history/.

16 For an interesting account of Harvard's relationship to the three books of Puritan education theology, see David Hill Scott, "A Vision of Veritas," *op cit*.

17 Purdom, Georgia. 2011. "Harvard: No Longer Truth for Christ and the Church," *Answers in Genesis*. https://answersingenesis.org/blogs/georgia-purdom/2011/10/11/harvard-no-longer-truth-for-christ-and-the-church/ (original link to the Harvard Graduate Christian Community website no longer active).

18 Ibid.

19 Mangalwadi, Vishal. "The Problem with The Bible Seminary: Sola Scriptura = Study only the Bible, A Paper Presented to the Faculty Forum The Gospel and Plow School of Theology," *Revelation Movement*. See also Mangalwadi's "Seminary: Education or Religious Schooling" in this book.

20 Stonestreet, John and G. Shane Morris. 2019. "The False God of Feelings: Mayor Buttigieg's Pro-Gay Christianity," *BreakPoint*. http://www.breakpoint.org/2019/04/breakpoint-the-false-god-of-feelings/.

21 See, for example, Romans 1:26–28, Jude 7–8, and 1 Timothy 1:8–11, among many others.

22 See Ryken, Leland J. 2010. *Worldly Saints: The Puritans as They Really Were*. Grand Rapids: Zondervan.

23 Scott, *op cit*.

24 Quoted in Keith L. Sprunger. 1972. *The Learned Doctor William Ames*. Eugene, OR: Wipf and Stock. 118.

25 Quoted in Overman, Christian. 2015. "The Basic Problem of the Christians. . . .," *Worldview Matters*. https://biblicalworldviewmatters.blogspot.com/2015/01/the-basic-problem-of-christians.html.

26 Adapted from David Hill Scott's essay "A Vision of Veritas: What Christian Scholarship Can Learn from the Puritan's 'Technology' of Integrating Truth," http://www.leaderu.com/aip/docs/scott.html.

27 Scott, *op cit*.

28 See Miller, Darrow. 2013. "Create Something on Earth to Hang on Heaven's Wall," *Darrow Miller and Friends*. http://darrowmillerandfriends.com/2013/04/04/create-something-on-earth-for-heaven/.

29 See the Lord's Prayer, Matthew 6:9–13 and Luke 11:1–4.

30 See "Firstfruits," BibleStudyTools.com, https://www.biblestudytools.com/dictionary/firstfruits/.

31 Adapted from David Hill Scott's essay "A Vision of Veritas: What Christian Scholarship Can Learn from the Puritan's 'Technology' of Integrating Truth," http://www.leaderu.com/aip/docs/scott.html.

32 Scott, *op cit.*
33 See the Westminster Shorter Catechism, http://www.westminsterconfession.org/confessional-standards/the-westminster-shorter-catechism.php.
34 At this moment in our history, we in the United States are following our European cousins and their atheistic pursuit of freedom *from* religion. On every side of our postmodern culture, there is a push to deny religious freedom and the corresponding freedoms of speech, thought, and assembly.
35 Webster, Daniel. *Webster's Dictionary* 1828 Online Edition. http://www.webstersdictionary1828.com/Quotes.
36 Ferguson, Niall. 2011. *Civilization: The West and the Rest.* New York: Penguin Books. 264.
37 Miller, Darrow. 2013. "The Atheists Who Honored the Bible," *Darrow Miller and Friends.* http://darrowmillerandfriends.com/2013/01/31/atheists-honored-bible/. See also http://darrowmillerandfriends.com/author/christian-overman/.
38 See her article *The Remarkable Role of the Bible in Early American Education* in this book.
39 See Tom Bloomer's paper on Calvin in Geneva in the resource section.
40 Sós, R. "'The City Upon A Hill' By John Winthrop: What Is It About?" *The Historic Present.* https://thehistoricpresent.com/2010/06/28/the-city-upon-a-hill-and-puritan-hubris/.
41 Miller, Darrow "The Education That Leads to Freedom," Disciple Nations Alliance, https://www.disciplenations.org/media/The-Education-That-Leads-to-Freedom_Miller3.pdf.
42 Ibid.
43 Overman, Christian. 2010. "The Missing Curriculum of God Centered Work," *Crosswalk.com.*
44 Ryken, Leland. 1990. *Worldly Saints: The Puritans as They Really Were.* Grand Rapids: Zondervan. 15.

Chapter Two

1 See unicef.org.
2 See globalissues.org.
3 See streetkids.net.
4 Berryman, Jerome. 2002. *The Complete Guide to Godly Play,* Vol. 1. Denver: Living the Good News. 112.
5 Slater, Rosalie. 1960. *Teaching and Learning America's Christian History: The Principle Approach.* San Francisco: Foundation for American Christian Education.
6 For a fuller teaching, see chapter 8 in *As the Family Goes, So Goes the Nation.*

Chapter Three

1 William Penn's vision for the education of children in the colony of Pennsylvania, Frame of Government, 1682.
2 Letter to John Adams, October 4, 1790.
3 Locke, John. 1690. *Thoughts on Education.*

4 Free online at http://webstersdictionary1828.com.

5 From the Preface of the print version of Webster's 1828 Dictionary.

6 *History of United States*, 1833 textbook by Noah Webster.

7 First Fruits of New England, a portion of Harvard College's Mission Statement, 1643.

8 Cremin, Lawrence A. 1970. *American Education: The Colonial Experience 1607–1783*. New York: HarperCollins. 40.

9 d'Aubigne, Jean-Henri Merle. 1846. *History of the Reformation in the Sixteenth Century*. Grand Rapids: Baker. 190.

10 The complete essay can be found online at: http://deila.dickinson.edu/cdm/fullbrowser/collection/ownwords/id/17784/rv/compoundobject/cpd/19843.

11 Sayers, Dorothy L. 1948. *The Lost Tools of Learning*. E.T. Heron. https://www.pccs.org/wp-content/uploads/2016/06/LostToolsOfLearning-DorothySayers.pdf.

12 http://deila.dickinson.edu/cdm/fullbrowser/collection/ownwords/id/17784/rv/compoundobject/cpd/19843.

13 This curriculum is available in four languages on the AMO® Program website http://amoprogram.com.

14 Slater, Rosalie. 1965. *Teaching and Learning America's Christian History: The Principle Approach*. San Francisco: Foundation for American Christian Education. xix.

15 Carson, Clarence. 1960. *The American Tradition*. The Foundation for Economic Education, Inc.

16 *Christian History*, Issue 50: Christianity and the American Revolution.

17 Hall, Verna. 1976. *Christian History of the American Revolution*. San Francisco: Foundation for American Christian Education.

18 Thornton, John Wingate. 1860. *The Pulpit of the American Revolution*. Reprinted by Bibliobazaar (2008). Preface.

19 Bancroft, George. 1875. *History of the United States of America from the Discovery of the Continent*, Vol. X. Boston: Little, Brown and Co. 310.

20 Adams, James Lewis. 1989. *Yankee Doodle Went to Church: The Righteous Revolution*. Revell.

21 Thornton, John Wingate. 1860. *The Pulpit of the American Revolution*. Reprinted by Bibliobazaar (2008). Preface.

22 Speech delivered in Boston, October 4, 1790.

23 Slater, Rosalie. 1965. *Teaching and Learning America's Christian History: The Principle Approach*. San Francisco: Foundation for American Christian Education. 19.

24 Hall, Verna, compiler. 1976. *The Christian History of the American Revolution: Consider and Ponder*. San Francisco: Foundation for American Christian Education. 606.

25 Ibid, 607.

26 William Howard Taft served as president for a four-year term followed by nine years as the tenth chief justice of the U.S. Supreme Court.

27 Ibid, 615.

Chapter Four

1 Higginbottom, Sam. 2016. *The Gospel and the Plow: The Old Gospel and Modern Farming in Ancient India*. Good Books.

2 See "Luther at the Imperial Diet of Worms (1521)," https://www.luther.de/en/worms.html

3 See Clark, Gordon H. "God and Logic," *The Trinity Foundation*. http://trinityfoundation.org/journal.php?id=16.

4 This summary is based on information from Vishal's publisher, YWAM Publishing, and other sources.

Chapter Five

1 I write as a U.S. citizen, but the story is similar in other nations influenced by the Reformation.

2 Other texts included The English Reader (1825), The National Reader (1828), The Young Scholar's Manual (1830), The National Spelling-Book (1858), and The American Preceptor (1811).

3 Hodge, A.A. 1887. *Popular Lectures on Theological Themes*. Presbyterian Board of Publication.

4 John Dewey (1859–1952) was the dominant voice of United States education in the twentieth century. A major advocate for so-called "progressive" education, and an outspoken atheist, Dewey was one of the signers of *Humanist Manifesto I,* in 1933. In his book, *A Common Faith,* Dewey spells out his "non-theistic faith." It is called "religious humanism."

5 Christian parents must also ask themselves if a "neutral" education is really what they want for their children. As Jonathan Lewis put it: "Neutrality isn't desirable even if it were possible." See Lewis' article, "The Neutrality Myths" in the July/Aug issue #82 of *Home School Enrichment* magazine.

6 I am indebted to Albert Wolters for similar ideas expressed in his book: Wolters, Albert. 1985. *Creation Regained: Biblical Basics for a Reformational Worldview*. Grand Rapids: Eerdmans.

7 "Segment: Wendell Berry on His Hopes for Humanity," November 29, 2013, https://billmoyers.com/segment/wendell-berry-on-his-hopes-for-humanity/.

8 Overman, Christian. 2012. *Assumptions That Affect Our Lives*. Bellevue, WA: Ablaze Publishing. 112–13. See http://www.biblicalworldview.com/bookstore.html.

9 See https://tnl.org/wp-content/uploads/Why-Work-Dorothy-Sayers.pdf.

10 Not only in Christian schools, but in churches as well, where SSD is perpetuated through the language that is often used, such as: "full-time Christian service," "clergy and laity," and the word "ministry" being reserved for work that pertains to the gathered church and its programs.

11 Shirer, William L. 1960. *The Rise and Fall of the Third Reich*. New York: Simon & Schuster. Chapter 8.

12 For excellent books connecting biblical worldview with vocation, see *LifeWork: A Biblical Theology for What You Do Every Day,* by Darrow Miller (Seattle: YWAM

Publishing) and *Biblical Worldview: Creation, Fall, Redemption*, edited by Mark L. Ward Jr. (Greenville, SC: BJU Press).

13 Bloom was born of second-generation Jewish immigrants.

14 Bloom, Allan. 1987. *The Closing of the American Mind: How Higher Education Has Failed Democracy and Impoverished the Souls of Today's Students*. New York: Simon & Schuster. 58.

15 Both quotes are from a letter written to David McClure, on October 25, 1836.

16 Warfel, Harry R. ed. 1953. *Letters of Noah Webster*. New York: Library Publishers. 453–57.

17 Miller, Darrow L. 2012. *LifeWork: A Biblical Theology for What You Do Every Day*. Seattle: YWAM Publishing.

18 Green, Albert, Jr. *Ten Touchstones of Distinctly Christian Thought*, 3, 10. Medina, WA: Alta Vista College.

19 Through His creation, God is not only speaking to those who believe in Him, but to non-believers as well, of every tribe and nation on earth. There is no place on earth where God's voice is not heard, nor any language group that does not understand it. See Romans 1:20, Psalm 19:1–4, and Psalm 97:6.

20 For more on Kuyper and this famous quote, see "The Postmodern Maze," Christian History Institute, https://christianhistoryinstitute.org/magazine/article/the-postmodern-maze.

21 Further evidence that Planet Earth was not given over to Satan at the Fall is in Genesis 9:1–3, where, after the flood, God tells Noah and his sons that every beast, fowl and fish will fear them. *"Into your hand they are given,"* God says. He didn't give them Satan's stuff. While Satan exerts temporary power in the earth, he does not own it.

22 Strandness, Erik L. 2014. *The Director's Cut: Finding God's Screenplay on the Cutting Room Floor*. Bloomington, IN: WestBow Press.

23 Wolters, Albert M. 1999. "The Foundational Command: 'Subdue the Earth,'" *Year of Jubilee, Cultural Mandate, Worldview*. Potchefstroom, South Africa: Institute for Reformational Studies. 27–34.

24 This fear is a bogeyman often described by the terms *dominion theology* and *dominionism*. These terms are attributed to sociologist Sara Diamond, who is said to have coined them in 1989. Yet, as Gagnon and Humphrey point out in the April 6, 2016, issue of *Christianity Today*, even Jewish journalist Stanley Kurtz has called this "conspiratorial nonsense." Lisa Miller called the accusation of dominionism "the paranoid *mot du jour*." Princeton's Robert George has said, "The contemporary religious Left's version of McCarthist red-baiting is to smear opponents by labeling them 'dominionists.'"

25 Scott, David Hill. "A Vision of Veritas: What Christian Scholarship Can Learn from the Puritan's [*sic*] 'Technology' of Integrating Truth," *LeadershipU*, http://www.leaderu.com/aip/docs/scott.html.

26 See Ryken, *op cit*.

27 Stevens, R. Paul. 2010. *The Other Six Days: Vocation, Work, and Ministry in Biblical Perspective*. Grand Rapids: Eerdmans.

28 Milton, John. "Of Education," https://www.dartmouth.edu/~milton/reading_room/of_education/text.shtml.

29 See Taylor, Justin. 2010. "The Only Christian Work Is Good Work Done Well unto God," *The Gospel Coalition*. https://www.thegospelcoalition.org/blogs/justin-taylor/the-only-christian-work-is-good-work-done-well-unto-god/.

30 Bakke, Ray. 1997. *A Theology as Big as the City*. Downers Grove: IVP. 34.

31 Erisman, Albert M. 2015. *The Accidental Executive: Lessons on Business, Faith, and Calling from the Life of Joseph*. Peabody, MA: Hendrickson Publishers.

32 Athenagoras. *A Plea Regarding Christians*. Quoted in Richardson, Cyril C., ed. 1996. *Early Christian Fathers*. New York: Touchstone. 310.

33 Willard, Dallas. 1988. *The Spirit of the Disciplines: Understanding How God Changes Lives*. New York: Harper Collins. 214.

34 See Dr. Jonathan T. Pennington's essay, *A Biblical Theology of Human Flourishing*, available through the Institute for Faith, Work & Economics at http://www.tifwe.org.

35 See http://biblicalworldview.com/Godspleasure.html.

36 The Puritans had their problems, but they got it right in more ways than they are commonly given credit. For more on this, see *Worldly Saints: The Puritans As They Really Were* by Leland Ryken. See also, *The Puritan Gift* by Ken and William Hopper. The Hopper brothers contend that the Puritan way brought about a level of business and economic flourishing in the United States the world had never seen before, that lasted for nearly 300 years.

Chapter Six

1 For more on this subject, we recommend Scott Allen's book *Why Social Justice Is Not Biblical Justice: An Urgent Appeal to Fellow Christians in a Time of Social Crisis* (Grand Rapids: Credo House Publishers, 2020). In this book, Scott refers to this religious worldview as "ideological social justice."

2 Philip Lancaster, *Family Man, Family Leader: Biblical Fatherhood as the Key to a Thriving Family* (San Antonio: The Vision Forum, Inc., 2003), 148.

Chapter Seven

1 This emphasis on the power of the human mind is often called Rationalism. It gave birth to the era called modernity, the condition of the last two or three centuries. For an authoritative summary of how modernity influenced the church and missions, see the chapter on the Enlightenment in Bosch, David. 1991. *Transforming Mission; Paradigm Shifts in Theology of Mission*. Maryknoll, New York: Orbis Books.

Disciple Nations Alliance (disciplenations.org) is an evangelical discipleship ministry whose vision is to train Christ-followers in an empowered, biblical worldview and equip them to be agents of Kingdom transformation, starting in their families, churches, communities, and vocations.

We invite you to explore our array of discipleship and training resources at disciplenations.org, and join the movement by becoming a "Kingdomizer" at disciplenations.org/kingdomizer.

If you'd like more information about any of our resources or opportunities, please contact us!

Disciple Nations Alliance
1110 E. Missouri Ave, Suite 393
Phoenix, AZ 85014
info@disciplenations.org
disciplenations.org